ANGEL
S T O R I E S

Angel Stories is an inspiring book of true-to-life testimonies by credible people who have experienced the God of the supernatural in their everyday lives. It might just help you become more aware that heavenly assistance is part of your divine inheritance!

—James W. Goll
Encounters Network
www.EncountersNetwork.com
Best-selling author, *The Seer*

Angels are all around us, yet they are rarely perceived. Angels are on assignment, yet their purpose is often misunderstood. Angels are mysterious, yet they leave indications of their reality for us to discover throughout our daily lives. You will be encouraged, inspired, and filled with faith as you read these angel stories from everyday people who have discovered this fascinating dimension of divine assistance. *Angel Stories* will give you hope to believe—and possibly even eyes to see into this often-unseen realm!

—Joshua Mills
New Wine International
www.JoshuaMills.com

Jonathan Nixon has hit it out of the park with his documentary and accompanying book *Angel Stories*. He intertwines real-life encounters with angels from the lives of some of the greatest revivalists of our time with mind-blowing revelation from the Scriptures. In doing so, Jonathan captures not only our imagination but also the simple reality that we probably are experiencing the supernatural unknowingly by entertaining angels unaware.

—Dennis Reanier
Revival Cry Ministries
www.RevivalCry.com

Jonathan Nixon has put together a fantastic collection of stories about unusual angelic visitations. This book will challenge you to believe. It will increase your faith to receive your own encounter!

—Katie Souza
Expected End Ministries
www.ExpectedEndMinistries.com

We are living in the most exciting time in history. Assistance from financial angels, healing angels, protection angels, breakthrough angels, and many other types of angels is increasing more and more today. It is amazing to watch what angels do to bring God's signs, wonders, and miracles to the earth. In this book Jonathan Nixon has compiled many incredible stories of how angels have impacted lives. God will use this book to open your eyes in a greater way to the activity of angelic beings around you.

—Joan Hunter
Joan Hunter Ministries
www.JoanHunter.org

I was blown away by Jonathan Nixon's incredible documentary film, *Angel Stories*, about the fascinating and life-changing encounters people have had with the angelic. Their amazing stories continue in this astonishing book.

—Robert John Grasseschi
Author, *The Catwalk to Christ*
www.RobertJohn.biz

Here are captivating encounters with the supernatural! *Angel Stories* reveals the amazing mission of angels through real-life stories that will surely encourage you and let you know that we are not alone!

—Doug Addison
Author, *Understand Your Dreams Now*
www.DougAddison.com

We are fortunate to be living in a time when the church is awakening to the supernatural ways of God and learning to live in awe and wonder of His omnipotence and glory. Studying God's ways makes us aware of how He moves supernaturally in our lives and the lives of others around us. As one of my spiritual fathers, John Paul Jackson, puts it, "What we focus on, we make room for." How can we set our focus on learning God's supernatural ways? By meditating on scriptures that teach us about the "supernaturalness" of our God and by reading testimonies like the ones shared in *Angel Stories* that bring to life what we are taught in God's Word. I highly recommend that you read this book and watch the DVD. You will be inspired, challenged, and, I believe, spurred to even greater reverence for Father God. For He is the Creator of angels and heavenly beings, the author of supernatural experiences, and the one who is due our honor and praise.

—Jeannine Rodriguez-Everard
Images of Light
www.ImagesofLight.us

ANGEL
STORIES

JONATHAN NIXON

CHARISMA
HOUSE

Most CHARISMA HOUSE BOOK GROUP products are available at special quantity discounts for bulk purchase for sales promotions, premiums, fund-raising, and educational needs. For details, write Charisma House Book Group, 600 Rinehart Road, Lake Mary, Florida 32746, or telephone (407) 333-0600.

ANGEL STORIES by Jonathan Nixon
Published by Charisma House
Charisma Media/Charisma House Book Group
600 Rinehart Road
Lake Mary, Florida 32746
www.charismahouse.com

Unless otherwise noted, all Scripture quotations are from the New King James Version of the Bible. Copyright © 1979, 1980, 1982 by Thomas Nelson, Inc., publishers. Used by permission.

Scripture quotations marked NAS are from the New American Standard Bible, copyright © 1960, 1962, 1963, 1968, 1971, 1972, 1973, 1975, 1977, 1995 by The Lockman Foundation. Used by permission. (www.Lockman.org)

Scripture quotations marked NIV are from the Holy Bible, New International Version. Copyright © 1973, 1978, 1984, International Bible Society. Used by permission.

Cover design by Lisa Rae Cox
Design Director: Bill Johnson

Visit the author's website at www.TentmakerFilmCompany.com.

Library of Congress Cataloging-in-Publication Data:
An application to register this book for cataloging has been submitted
to the Library of Congress.
International Standard Book Number: 978-1-62136-552-5
E-book ISBN: 978-1-62136-553-2

AUTHOR'S NOTE: All testimonies have been published with
written permission.

This publication is translated in Spanish under the title *Historias
de ángeles*, copyright © 2014 by Jonathan Nixon, published by Casa
Creación, a Charisma Media company. All rights reserved.

First edition

14 15 16 17 18 — 9 8 7 6 5 4 3 2 1
Printed in the United States of America

CONTENTS

ANGELS ARE REAL

By Jonathan Nixon

H AVE YOU EVER sensed the presence of angels? Have you ever seen an angel? In his book *Angels: God's Secret Agents*, evangelist Billy Graham shares an interesting story about John G. Paton, who served as a missionary in the South Pacific in the early 1800s:

> Hostile natives surrounded his mission headquarters one night, intent on burning the Patons out and killing them. John Paton and his wife prayed all during that terror-filled night that God would deliver them. When daylight came they were amazed to see that, unaccountably, the attackers had left. They thanked God for delivering them.
>
> A year later, the chief of the tribe was converted to Jesus Christ, and Mr. Paton, remembering what had happened, asked the chief what had kept him and his men from burning down the house and killing them. The chief replied in surprise, "Who were all those men you had with you there?" The missionary answered, "There were no men there; just my wife and I." The chief argued that they had seen many men standing guard—hundreds of big men in shining garments with drawn swords in their hands. They seemed to circle the mission station so that the natives were afraid to attack.*

"Could it be that God had sent a legion of angels to protect His servants, whose lives were being endangered?" Graham asks. Indeed. Could it be? Are angels real? Or is this story and the others in this book just the ravings of devout lunatics?

---

* Billy Graham, *Angels: God's Secret Agents* (London: Hodder & Stoughton, 1976), 12–13.

Our culture has a fascination with the supernatural. The biggest summer blockbuster movies often feature superheroes with supernatural powers, and TV is filled with paranormal programming. There is even a TV series titled *Supernatural*. And I haven't even mentioned the popular interest in ESP, aliens, UFOs, contacting "the other side," and tracking ghosts. The occult is now passé. Fortune-telling, Ouija boards, tarot cards, white magic, wizards and warlocks, and the like are now openly embraced in our culture. Yet many people still can't wrap their heads around angels.

Why do people so easily accept the dark side of the supernatural but have such a hard time believing God made heavenly creatures to assist us? After all, references to angels in the Bible far outnumber references to Satan and his demons.

Hebrews 1:14 tells us that God sends forth "ministering spirits...to minister for those who will inherit salvation." My prayer is that the stories in this book will encourage you to truly believe there are awesome, mighty, supernatural beings to guard, protect, and assist you—right now!

I have no trouble believing in angels. I believe in angels because the Bible says angels exist, and I believe the Bible to be the true Word of God. I also believe in angels because I have sensed their presence around me. I have felt the wind from their wings, I have smelled their heavenly fragrance, and I have on occasion even seen them move as flashes of light as they go about their kingdom business on my behalf.

Spiritual forces and resources are available to all Christians. Millions of angels are at God's command and at our service. The hosts of heaven stand at attention, and Satan and his fallen angels are no match for God's heavy artillery. God has "disarmed principalities and powers," according to Colossians 2:15, making "a public spectacle of them, triumphing over them in it."

If the activities of the devil and his demons seem to be intensifying in our culture, should we not realize that God's angels are also on assignment? Christians must never fail to sense the operation of God's angelic messengers. We should realize that God's heavenly hosts far eclipse Satan's kingdom.

Rather than thinking of how busy the devil's minions are, we should be more alert to the fact that angels are working all around us. We should realize that powerful angels are accompanying us on our life experiences.

I pray that your awareness of angelic intervention will be heightened after you read this book. I pray you will be reminded that God loves you as you see how He has sent His mighty angels to protect and assist His children. Look up and take courage. "For He shall give His angels charge over you, to keep you in all your ways. In their hands they shall bear you up, lest you dash your foot against a stone" (Ps. 91:11–13). God has not left you to go through life all alone. Angels are nearer than you think.

PART 1

ANGELS ON ASSIGNMENT

Do not forget to entertain strangers, for by so doing
some have unwittingly entertained angels.
—Hebrews 13:2

THE SUPERNATURAL IS REAL

By Randy Clark

WHEN I WAS in seminary, a NASA scientist spoke to my class and said this: "We only live in the three dimensions that we perceive, but I believe, and I believe that science indicates, that there are other dimensions that occupy the same space continuum in which we live. We cannot perceive, see, or enter into those dimensions, but they are there."

This helps us understand where heaven is. It's not that heaven is "way out there" somewhere in space; it is literally in another dimension, a spiritual dimension.

Angels, who were created and exist in this other dimension, can move out of the spirit dimension into ours. They can manifest themselves and be seen, or they can choose not to be seen.

Angels are assigned to carry out God's purposes. They watch over His words to perform them, they work with us, and they are a part of the host of heaven to worship God. These are their main purposes: to worship God and to serve those of us who have eternal life. The psalmist tells us that angels watch over His Word, performing the voice of His Word (Ps. 103:20–21), and in the Book of Hebrews, chapter 1, we read, "Are not all angels ministering spirits sent to serve those who will inherit salvation?" (v. 14, NIV).

It is interesting to note that Christianity, Judaism, Islam, and Hinduism, all of the major religions of the world throughout time, believe in both the demonic and the angelic. Both the demonic spirits and the angelic beings were created by God. They are not eternal because they have a beginning. God is eternal because He has no beginning and no end, while angels were created by God and therefore have a beginning. I believe that God created them before He created the physical realm, our universe. They were created and exist in the spirit realm.

They were all created to worship Him and to carry out His

purposes. But a third of the angels "fell," meaning they lost favor with God because of rebellion, and are no longer able to come into the presence of God. The common understanding is that these fallen angels are demons.

I understand this now, but when I graduated from seminary, I didn't believe in the supernatural. My training was in liberal theology. In college I majored in religion, and in seminary I was taught liberal theology. A liberal worldview doesn't allow for supernatural things. So when I graduated from seminary, I didn't believe in demons. I didn't believe in them *until* I had one talk to me through one of my parishioners, until I saw it distort the person's face and do grotesque things. And for me it was that classic "aha" moment. All of a sudden, with that personal experience, my liberal theology went out the window. I said, "This is really real!"

I have friends who can literally see angels, and I have experienced many supernatural things. I've been in meetings where I was pushed off balance by an angel, where I almost fell over, but when I turned around no one was there.

Once when I was ministering in Brazil with an associate, as I looked at him, suddenly it seemed like somebody turned on a bright light behind him. There was a crowd of people there who also saw it with their natural eyes. They saw these rays of light going out of his body. And that's when miracles started happening all over the place—even without this minister praying for anybody.

I've talked with people who have had out-of-body experiences and seen the Lord and been used to bring great miracles—creative miracles such as broken bones going back into place, just like that, and cancers totally disappearing in an instant. When you have seen those things happen, then healing is easy to believe in. And when you have seen the effect of demons destroying people's lives, and seen them manifest right in front of you, once that happens, you no longer have any doubt that the supernatural is real.

An international evangelist and healing minister, Randy Clark is the founder of Global Awakening Ministries (www.GlobalAwakening .com). After following a call to ministry in 1970, he went on to pastor for thirty years, spending half of that time as senior pastor of Vineyard Christian Fellowship in St. Louis, Missouri. His life was forever changed on January 20, 1994, when he walked into a small storefront church near the Toronto, Ontario, airport. Originally scheduled to last four days, the meetings turned into a worldwide revival that has impacted millions of people. Clark holds a master's degree in divinity from Southern Baptist Theological Seminary and a doctor of ministry from United Theological Seminary. He resides in Mechanicsburg, Pennsylvania, with his wife, DeAnne. They have four adult children.

THE ANGEL IN THE FLANNEL SHIRT

By Jeannine Rodriguez-Everard

As I was flying into Denver International Airport after being away for Christmas, I realized I had no idea where I'd parked my car. I had pulled into one of those long-term lots, which are huge in Denver—absolutely *huge*. So as the plane was landing, I was praying, "God, could You just remind me where I parked?" I was thinking, "I teach people how to hear God's voice. So you'd think He could tell me where my car is parked!"

But I was getting nothing.

When I boarded the shuttle bus for long-term parking, a guy sat down in front of me. He was wearing a flannel shirt and jeans. And he turned around right away and looked at me—and winked! It wasn't a flirtatious wink; it was more like he was telling me, "I know something you don't know."

But then he got into a conversation with someone else, and I saw a friend of mine on the bus and started talking too. But as I was talking with my friend, I could overhear his conversation in front of me. He was saying that he'd been in Michigan for a couple of weeks.

Well, as we approached the long-term lot, I still had absolutely no clue where my car was. So I decided I would get off at the first stop and just walk around and see what happened. Maybe I'd have to keep getting on and off the bus—just keep riding it until I found my car.

When I get off at the first stop, the guy in the flannel shirt got off at the same time. Now, I've just come home after being away for Christmas, and I am loaded down with bags, gifts, and all kinds of stuff—loads of stuff—and right away the guy said to me, "Are you looking for your car?"

"Yeah," I answered, "but I have absolutely no idea where I parked it."

"Well, you know what," he said, "my car is parked right over here. Why don't I give you a lift, and we'll just go find your car?"

Now, I would never normally get into a car with a stranger. But I just had this feeling that I could trust him. So he took all my bags, and as I was getting into his car, I half-noticed that his car was unlocked. As he's putting all my bags and other stuff in the back, I sort of noticed that he wasn't wearing a coat—remembering that he said he'd been in Michigan. And then I was conscious of the fact that he didn't have any of his own luggage. Nothing. But still, I was focused on finding my car and wasn't really thinking too much about any of that. None of it really had registered yet.

As he got in and started to drive, he said, "You know what? I have a sense your car is over in this other area of the parking lot."

So he drove there, and sure enough he drove me right to my car. He got out, pulled all my luggage out, and put it into my car. And I'm like, "Um, thanks. I mean, thank you *so* much." It was just so easy—he simply drove to the other part of the garage, and there was my car.

When all my stuff was in my car, I asked, "What's your name?"

"Oh, my name is Brad."

"Oh, I'm Jeannine. Thank you so much. I can't even, you know, thank you enough."

As I got into my car, he drove away—and all of a sudden it hit me! That was an angel!

I sat in my car—didn't drive—just sat there and began thinking back over all the details. He said he'd been in Michigan for two weeks over Christmas, but he had no coat. He was wearing only jeans and a flannel shirt. He had no luggage with him, even though he said he'd been away for two weeks. His car was parked right at the shuttle-bus stop, and it was unlocked. He drove me directly to my car—like, *straight* to my car. On the bus he'd sat down right in front of me, turned around and winked—which is when I realized the very last thing he did before saying good-bye, after he put my bags in my car and I thanked him, was give me that wink again! It was like he was saying, "I know something you don't know."

I knew in that moment he was an angel! God had sent an angel to help me out. He just looked like a normal guy—very human, normal voice and everything else. He didn't glow; he just looked normal.

But—and this is what amazed me and touched me the most in that moment—even though I had always thought my first angelic encounter would be a major event with blinding, flashing white lights and some extreme message from God, it was a moment of personal need when the Lord just showed His concern for me. It was cold, dark, and late that night flying into Denver, and the long-term parking lot was huge. And God just wanted to help me out because I didn't know where my I'd parked my car. So He sent an *angel* to help me out.

Jeannine Rodriguez-Everard is an artist, singer, and Bible teacher. The founder of Images of Light (www.ImagesOfLight.us), she has a passion for teaching people to bring heaven to earth through intimacy with God. As a trainer with Streams Ministries International, the ministry of prophetic teacher John Paul Jackson, she also leads prophetic evangelism teams that minister at film and arts festivals, New Age gatherings, and in everyday settings. She and her husband, Ian, live in Hove, England.

THE RESCUE ANGEL

By Randy DeMain

Years ago I was in Saigon, Vietnam, with a humanitarian aid group. We had been there about fourteen days, and I was ready to go home. On the way to the airport I had my airline ticket in my front shirt pocket. When I arrived, I got off the bus and entered the busy terminal to check in for my flight. People were everywhere. Somehow amid the crowds and all the bustling and jostling, I ended up inside the terminal with no ticket.

I checked and double-checked but nothing. No ticket.

I went into a mild panic; I was just *so* ready to be home. I went straight to the ticket counter and told the agent, "I've lost my ticket." I was sure he could look up my name on his computer and see that I did indeed have a ticket, and then print a duplicate for me to use to board the plane.

Unfortunately this was during the late 1990s when Vietnam was under a trade embargo and the airports there had little to no computer service. The airline agent had no ability to access my flight itinerary or ticket information.

He said, "I'm sorry, sir, I have no record of your flight or ticket. That will be $2,500 for your return flight home."

I was aghast.

"You said $2,500? Do you take credit cards?"

"No, sir. That's going to have to be cash."

Immediately I thought, "OK, I'm stuck. I'm stuck in Vietnam."

I went over to the group of guys I was traveling with and told them, "We've got to do something. I'm stuck here. I've lost my ticket. I'm sure it was pilfered from my pocket on the way in."

So they all gathered around for a couple of minutes—a dozen guys huddled together. I prayed aloud, "Lord, I need my ticket home. Can You please tell me where to find it or restore this ticket?"

Then all the guys just dispersed and started looking around the airport for the ticket.

I turned around and had walked only about five steps when a man, a Vietnamese man, walked straight up to me and said, "Here's your ticket." I grabbed it and looked at it excitedly. And there, in fact, were my name and the day's date. They were my tickets! So I looked up to thank this gentleman, but he was not there. He was gone. Disappeared, literally.

Suddenly it dawned on me that this guy had been dressed in absolutely clean, perfectly pressed brown khaki shorts and a brown khaki shirt. He spoke to me in perfect English, with no Asian accent whatsoever. I knew he was indeed an angel and had brought me a new set of tickets, right there in the airport!

In all my experiences over the years I have had a couple of encounters with messenger angels, but that day in Vietnam I met a rescue angel!

The founder of Kingdom Revelation Ministries (www.Kingdom Revelation.org), Randy DeMain is an apostolic revivalist who has been preaching the gospel for more than twenty-five years to see the body of Christ touch the world by demonstrating the power of God. A former pastor, teacher, and church planter, he regularly conducts evangelism and healing crusades, teaches at training events, and speaks at conferences worldwide.

ANGELS SITTING ON YOUR SHOULDERS

By Dennis Reanier

WHILE I WAS attending a conference in Missoula, Montana, I saw a woman who the Lord showed me had angels sitting on her shoulders. I told her, "I see two angels sitting on your shoulders, one on each shoulder."

The friends who were with her were not believers, and they actually responded to what I said by swearing! That was probably the correct response for them, because the supernatural was not something they were aware of.

But I had a prophetic word for this woman, and the Holy Spirit led me to say to her: "You have been abused, and you have been through all kinds of physical and even sexual abuse. But the Lord has shown me that God is going to use you to rescue women out of the same kinds of situations that you have come out of."

Well, I found out the next day that this woman had been chained up in a basement and sexually abused for ten years and had escaped and been saved only two weeks before the conference. She had since entered Teen Challenge, and God was redeeming her life. Her heart was for God to send her to the nations to rescue other women from the sex trade. The prophetic word confirmed two things, actually three, for her: that God was redeeming her life and would use her— and that He had assigned two angels to her.

Dennis Reanier is the founder of the Apostolic Resource Center, Revival Cry Ministries (www.RevivalCry.com), and LOFT in Bozeman, Montana. He is also the cofounder of Be a Hero, USA—a nonprofit organization that helps at-risk children around the world. The author of Shaking Heaven and Earth, *he seeks to mobilize people to be catalysts for revival, reformation, and renewal to prepare for the end-times harvest. He and his wife, Tammi, live in Bozeman, Montana, with their four daughters.*

ANGELS DELIVER NEW BODY PARTS

By Joan Hunter

THE BIBLE HAS so much to say about angels. We are living in the time of revelation, and there are more angelic beings and visions being released to earth and to us than ever before. We just need to be aware of them. We just need to acknowledge them by saying: "God, I thank You; thank You that healing angels are being released, that financial angels are being released"—and it is amazing what God does.

In fact, in a service once when I saw an angel for the very first time with my physical eyes, I thought at first I was looking at a cloud, like a glory cloud. I rubbed my eyes, trying to figure it out. I thought, "What is that? Am I having a weird vision, or is this my imagination?" I couldn't really tell. It's like that the first time you see something you aren't familiar with.

These angels were going over the congregation, over the people in the church, and I was seeing them, but they looked kind of weird to me. And "weird" is really an understatement, but it is the only way I can describe them. These angels didn't have wings; they had an arm span. They were gliding, like flying, over the congregation, and each of them had a big hump on his back. I couldn't figure it out; I couldn't make out what that hump was. It was like I was seeing deformed angels, but I'd never seen or heard of that.

Then, suddenly I said, "In the name of Jesus, somebody over here needs a heart. In the name of Jesus I send the word of healing. I send a new heart in Jesus's name." And instantly I saw this angel reach backward into the hump, and at that moment the person I was praying for moved abruptly as if he had been hit by something. In that moment he received a brand-new heart.

The humps on the backs of the angels were like backpacks. There were body parts in there! God showed me He had body parts for the people in the service. "This is awesome!" I thought.

So I just kept going, and I just kept praying. I saw a man and said, "New lungs," and the angel reached behind into the hump and the man got new lungs! We all saw him react like he'd been hit! He took a really deep breath—haaa—and said, "I can breathe!"

That's how the night went. It was *way* cool!

These are my healing angels. They are healing angels God has sent to travel with me, and they bring fresh body parts from heaven—every time. It's awesome.

People who have had experiences going to heaven sometimes report that there are warehouses full of body parts. My position is that I do not want any body part left in the heavenly warehouse! As for anyone who comes to my service, I want them to get their new body part; that's for sure. And God just does it.

He has given knees, elbows, lungs, shoulders, hearts, prostates, intestines, even a back. One person received the part of their colon that had been taken out. It is just awesome.

I don't know how God does it. I just know that He does.

That first time I saw the angels gliding over the congregation, reaching into the humps on their backs and delivering new body parts, also was my first experience personally ministering with and seeing these angels. But now they go with me wherever I go; and when I am praying, anointing, and imparting, there is an infusion of the anointing power of healing, and God sends the healing angels.

Joan Hunter committed her life to Christ at age twelve and began serving in ministry alongside her parents, Charles and Frances Hunter, who traveled the globe conducting Healing Explosions and Healing Schools. Today she is a teacher, author, and healing evangelist in her own right. As founder and president of Texas-based Joan Hunter Ministries (www. JoanHunter.org), Hearts 4 Him, 4 Corners Foundation, and 4 Corners World Outreach Center, she seeks to equip believers to take the healing power of God to the four corners of the earth. The author of three books— Healing the Whole Man Handbook, Healing the Heart, *and* Power to Heal—*she lives with her husband in Pinehurst, Texas.*

AN ANGEL WITH A PICKAX

By Joan Hunter

I REMEMBER ONE TIME praying over finances, specifically over the finances of the congregation. I looked at a particular person and thought, "This is really strange. He has something in his hand, but I don't recognize what it is." I was seeing in the spirit a vision of something in his hands. He wasn't physically holding it, but I could see in the spirit a tool in his hands. But I'm a city girl not a country girl, so I didn't know what the tool was. I began to describe the tool, and the person said, "That's a pickax you're seeing."

Then I saw these really big angels, and one of them used a pickax to hit rocks in front of this person, as if there was a dam in front of him and the angel was using the pickax to smash the rocks. A little trickle was coming out of the rocks; the angel was destroying the dam that had held back the person's finances.

Next I saw huge angel hands. They reached inside the dam and came out with wads—and I mean huge handfuls—of cash. Just as if they were reaching into a bank vault, the huge hands were coming out with handfuls of cash. I prophesied what I was seeing, over and over. I saw these finance angels go to four people in the congregation. As it turned out, all four had had money withheld from them and lost money in their businesses. God began to restore finances to them.

Sometime later I was ministering at another church when I remembered the finance angels. I was going to share the story with the people there, but right as I was about to get up to do that, my daughter Melody said, "Mom, I'm seeing angels up at the front, and they have this big thing, this big tool in their hand."

Melody was not at the earlier meeting and had not heard me talk about the encounter with the pickax angels. So I shared with her about the encounter, and she said, "That's what I'm seeing. These angels are doing this"—and she moved her arms up and down as if she were hitting the ground with a pickax.

But the really great part was that suddenly more angels arrived and gave the angel with the pickax a wad of dynamite to blow up all the hindrances and all the dams—to blow up anything that had held back Christ's finances from the people. The hindrances were completely obliterated, and finances were able to flow. They could now flow like a river.

God wants to use us as a river of finances, and what's awesome about a river of finances is that along the riverside are *banks*! And the banks are full too! So we can have money in the bank, and we can also help fund the kingdom of God.

Hallelujah! I like those financial angels!

LUNCH WITH AN ANGEL

By John Paul Jackson

A NGELS ARE CREATED beings. There are warring angels, ministering angels, and angels sent specifically to protect us. There
are lots of different kinds of angels, but they really have only one
purpose, and that is to help us.

Some people think an angel's job is to defend God. But God
does not need defending. If God were to raise His little finger, then
boom!—whatever He wanted, it would be done. God just thinks a
thought, and it's done. God does not need defending.

Angels are here to help *us*. They are the links between heaven
and earth. God's Spirit reveals Himself to us, and His angels are
His logistic agents. So they help us get from one place to another.
They protect us from certain things and events. They protect us
from things that the enemy (Satan) wants to happen. Our goal is to
live a life that allows God to be justified in sending them to help us.

Some angels are sent to help other angels. For example, angels
could be sent to help the angel who has been assigned to you. Some
people have more than one angel because of the callings God has
on their lives and because of the difficulty of what they are going
through or will be going through.

The angels personally assigned to us for life are with us for all
of our lives. When angels are assigned to us, they often take on
an appearance like ours and look like us. In fact, angels who are
assigned to children often will take the form of a child when they
are assigned to a child.

We know angels can look like us because of the story in the New
Testament when Peter was freed from jail and went to the house of
Mary (Acts 12:5–18). When he arrived and knocked, the servant
girl Rhoda opened the door and on seeing Peter thought it was his
angel, because she knew Peter was in jail.

The only logical conclusion we can take from her reaction is that it was commonly known among the early believers that angels looked like the person they were assigned to. Otherwise there's no explanation for why Rhoda would think she saw Peter's angel and not Peter himself.

We also know angels can look like humans because the Bible tells us we can be unaware we are entertaining angels (Heb. 13:2). How could we be unaware we are entertaining angels unless it's because they look like people?

So we know from Scripture that angels can look like humans, or they can come in the glory of heaven—which is when, as many Bible stories say, we melt at their feet like dead men.

For example, when the angels appeared to Daniel, he fell at their feet. John also fell at the feet of the angel who came to him. This is because those angels didn't come as men; they came in their heavenly glory.

But when they come in human forms, we can actually ask them to lunch! Abraham did this. When the Lord and two angels came to talk with Abraham, Abraham invited them to lunch, and they stayed. The Lord and His two angels sat down and ate with Abraham.

Considered an authority on dream interpretation, John Paul Jackson is a respected Bible teacher and founder of Streams Ministries International (www.StreamsMinistries.com) based near Dallas, Texas. His simple yet profound "explanations of the unexplainable" help people relate to God and one another in fresh ways. An author, speaker, and television guest, John Paul ministers to an international audience through the courses and publications of the Streams Training Center.

ANGELS DON'T ASK
FOR MY OPINION

By John Paul Jackson

H UMANS ABSOLUTELY CAN interact with angels, but it's very interesting—I've had several encounters with angels, but not once have they asked my opinion. Not once! When angels come to me, they usually do so to tell me what needs to happen. They come with a message or a direction.

Only one time when an angel came to me and talked with me about something I needed to do did he actually talk with me about something I wanted to know. That time, while the angel was telling me what I needed to do, I had a question in my mind about a certain individual. When the angel had completed his instruction, he started walking out the door, then turned around and looked back at me and said, "Oh, concerning this individual (and named the person), I will be back on July 24 to tell you about that."

By July 24 I had completely forgotten that he said he'd be back. I went to sleep that night as usual but was awakened in the middle of the night. When I woke up, the same angel was standing there and said, "Now, here's what you need to know about this individual."

HITCHHIKING WITH AN ANGEL

By John Paul Jackson

ONE TIME I bought a pickup truck, and it was just one of those things for me—it was my dream vehicle. I *really* wanted it. I told myself, "God wants me to have it. I'm going to save my money, and when I get enough money, I'll be able to buy this pickup truck." At the time I just loved trucks, so when I saw this particular pickup in the paper—and it was a really great price, like $3,000 below wholesale—I thought, "This is it!"

But first a little backstory. I had a friend who had seen a Mercedes-Benz for sale in the paper for $500. He went to the woman who advertised it and said, "I know this has to be a mistake. I know you're really selling it for $50,000." But she said, "No. It really is $500." When he asked her what was wrong with it, she said, "Nothing. It's perfect. It's in mint condition, but my husband has run away with his secretary and has told me to sell the car and send him the money I get for it. So I'm selling the car for $500, and I'm going to send him the money."

So when I saw the pickup truck in the paper for $3,000 under wholesale, I thought, "This is like that! I'm going to get this truck!" I went to look it over, and it was all shiny and clean. It had everything that I wanted. So I paid the money and got the truck.

I decided to drive it to West Texas where I was invited to speak at a church. At one point I'd driven so far I hadn't seen anything for twenty miles. Not even a cow. It was desolate. Nothing is going on. And that's when my truck started slowing down. I pushed on the gas, but it slowed down to nothing. I looked in the mirror and saw smoke billowing out from under the truck, and I realized I had blown the transmission. It had burned up. And there I am in the middle of desolate West Texas. There was nothing and no one.

20

"Lord," I asked, "why did You allow this to happen? I'm Your servant. I am going to speak at this church. I have to be there tonight. I'm speaking tonight. Why are You letting this happen to me?"

And the Lord spoke back to me. He said, "I didn't tell you to buy this truck."

"But Lord," I answered, "it was the right price. It was everything I wanted."

"I didn't tell you to buy this truck," He repeated.

"Well, Lord, OK, I'm sorry. I am. I'm sorry I bought it," I replied. "But, Lord, help me. I have got to be at the church tonight. Please help me."

I had not even finished praying that prayer when over a little rise in the road came an old, old, like 1960s, car. It was just puttering along. A man was driving who looked like a farmer. He stopped, looked at me, and said, "Boy, it's not your lucky day is it?"

"No, sir, it's not," I said. "I made a mistake buying this truck."

"Well, I reckon you did," he said. "Where are you going?"

"You don't know the place," I told him, assuming he wouldn't. "I'm going to this little town called Floydada, Texas."

"I know exactly where it's at," he said. "I'm going right through there, son. Hop in, and I'll take you."

So I got in, and he drove me to Floydada, Texas. He dropped me off at the church, and when I get out of his car, I took two steps up onto the sidewalk and turned around to thank him, and...he was gone.

I mean, the car was gone. The man was gone. There was nothing. The car wasn't driving away; it was just gone. Two seconds, two steps. He was gone.

I had entertained an angel "unaware," as the Scripture says—until that very moment when I looked back and realized, "Oh my goodness. That was an angel."

I PUT MY ANGELS TO WORK

By Doug Addison

WHEN I WAS in South Africa in 2009, the angelic encounters I had were amazing and powerful. I noticed on the very first day I returned home to California that their presence was still very strong. I was having amazing quiet times and getting revelation.

A few days into this I asked the Lord, "What do I do?"—because I sensed that these angels I had encountered in South Africa were now with me in California.

The Lord answered, "Well, put them to work."

I didn't even know you could do that!

So I made a list. I really prayed about it for a day, then made my list and asked God to do it. Through the Holy Spirit I asked the Lord to assign these angels to the tasks.

The next day when I woke up, no angels were in my house. It was almost as if I felt cold; I could feel their absence.

I asked the Lord, "Where are all the angels?"

The Holy Spirit answered me, "Well, you put them to work. That's why they're not here."

That was when I really began to understand about angels. They actually do have to come and to go.

About a week later I was going through a really difficult time. One night, in the middle of the night, I could feel the presence of the angels again in my bedroom. I sat up in bed and asked them, "Why are you here? What is going on?"

I couldn't see them, but I could feel their presence. I could see a light, just out of the corner of my eye, but the angels spoke directly into my spirit and said, "We do not have an assignment for you right now. You are moving into a new season in your life, and we do not have an assignment to protect you. What we are doing is doubling up on assignments and rendezvousing in your bedroom at night."

"Wow, this is interesting," I thought.

For about two months I received revelation—so much revelation— simply because these angels were rendezvousing in my bedroom at night. It was funny; I'd wake up and blurt out, "There's something new in Detroit. What is it?"—things like that. I'd ask about something without knowing what it was about, but I would know of it because the angels were rendezvousing in my bedroom in the middle of the night.

Doug Addison (www.DougAddison.com) is a frequent conference speaker who captivates international audiences with clean stand-up comedy and high-energy prophetic ministry. He is also the award-winning author of seven books, including Personal Development God's Way *and* Understand Your Dreams Now: Spiritual Dream Interpretation. *He and his wife, Linda, live in Los Angeles, California.*

WAS IT A VISION OR WAS IT REAL?

By Doug Addison

WHEN I WAS in South Africa, we had five days of spiritual encounters that were very powerful. After our meetings I would go back to my room and be up half the night, or I would be taken places in the spirit.

One night I had an encounter that was a lot like the one explained in Acts 12:5–18, when Peter didn't know if he was seeing a vision or if the angel was real. For me it was the same way; I didn't know if I was having a vision or if I was actually experiencing the events.

On that night I went back to my room after the meetings and lay down on my bed. Suddenly, in real time, I was back in California—just like that. I was driving down the 101 Highway in my town where I live. I was trying to figure out if this was really happening to me or if I was dreaming or if I was seeing a vision. It felt completely real!

As I'm driving down the 101, I look over and see workers with Caltrans, the state transportation department, on the side of the road all bent over at a forty-five-degree angle scooping up things and putting them into bags. These workers—there were about twelve of them—all turned their heads at the same time, looked directly at me, and locked eyes with me. In that moment their faces turned into angelic faces with red eyes.

Instantly the fear of God hit me.

Then they all went back to work, their faces turned back down, and I could see they were scooping balls of white light. The Holy Spirit showed me that these were gathering angels; they were gathering balls of white light at the side of the freeway, and I could see that the balls of light were the souls of people. These balls were the people who had been "discarded off to the side of the road." They had been overlooked or wounded by the church, but these gathering angels had come to scoop them up.

After that I found myself back in my own home in California, and I was shaking because the presence of God was so strong. My front doorbell rang, and I answered the door to find two angels standing there. One of them was dressed like a jester, and the other had work clothes on.

It was so strange to see that I had to really pray into that vision to understand it. The Holy Spirit showed me that the angel wearing the work clothes was assigned to me to get things done. The other was a comedy angel—which for me makes sense because I do stand-up comedy as a means of sharing God's love.

In fact, it was right after this encounter that my comedy went to a whole new and different level and people would be healed at events when I did my stand-up routine. That was the result of this angelic encounter.

Then, when that encounter was over, I was back again in my room in South Africa.

NOW YOU SEE THEM, NOW YOU DON'T

By Doug Addison

ONE NIGHT I asked some angels who were coming to my room regularly, "Why don't you show yourselves?" Sometimes I could see them and sometimes I couldn't. So I asked them, "Why don't you show yourselves now or in meetings when you are there?"

Their answer came with a real sternness. I was told, "We have come from heaven. We have been sent by the Father, through the Holy Spirit, to bring revelation or to bring a message. If we show ourselves, we distract from that revelation or from that message. Therefore, we normally stay cloaked."

And that's why you sometimes can see an angel and other times you don't even know they are there. But know this: whether you see them or not, they are always there.

THE MEDIATION ANGEL

By Doug Addison

I WAS PRAYING ONE morning—it was a normal morning in which I'd get up and start praying—but suddenly the presence of God increased, and I knew it was because angels had come into the room. I've learned what it feels like when angels show up. I've been able to start discerning it because I take notes and journal all my experiences. So I knew angels had come into the room with the Holy Spirit.

Then the Holy Spirit told me, "Speak things out that have been promised to you. Call them into being; decree them over your life."

So I did. I went on for a half hour with authority, walking back and forth, decreeing over my life different promises and prophecies that had been spoken to me. I was breaking into a sweat because I was so engaged in the act. Time stood still. It was a supernatural encounter with God.

When I finished, I was going to take a shower because I had really worked up a sweat, but suddenly right there in front of me appeared a parchment of paper, like an ancient, gold-trimmed, bronze-looking piece of paper. It appeared in midair and then floated down to the floor and disappeared. I was really taken by surprise and said out loud, "Whoa! What was that?"

The Lord spoke to me and said, "That was a decree from heaven." Apparently because I had decreed things on earth as they are in heaven, what I decreed actually was being released. The things I decreed were being released to me and to other people. The Lord told me He was releasing decrees from heaven right then, and He was also releasing the angels to go along with them to help bring those things about. It was the things that we have been called to do, and He was dispatching heavenly resources.

Right after this I called an attorney friend of mine to find out more about decrees. I learned that in court when you file a motion requesting certain things, if the judge issues an order in your favor, then the order has a decree in it. That decree is the part of the order that authorizes and requires the request to be fulfilled.

Not long after this I went to sleep one night and had a dream. In it I was praying a prayer that was really a complaint. It was a legitimate complaint against the publisher of my book. The publisher had gone out of business, which meant my book was caught up in the process and stuck, unable to be published. I was really upset about it. As I began to pray in the dream, I was taken by an angel to the courtroom of heaven.

Now I had never really seen this, but it looked like a regular, but giant, courtroom, and it was jam-packed. There were so many people filing motions against each other. They all were Christians, all complaining and filing motions against other Christians. The place was so jam-packed, and the angels assigned to each case were running low, low on energy and low on resources.

The angel showing this to me said, "This is what's going on in the courtroom of heaven. Many Christians are accusing other Christians, and they were tapping out the resources of heaven."

So the angel asked me, "Would you be willing to settle your complaint out of court?" I was there to complain as well, so I said, "By all means, yes, I will settle out of court."

I woke up at that point, but a week later I had another dream. In that dream the same angel, who is a mediating angel, sat down with me and with the publisher and we actually worked it out; we mediated the situation between us—all in the dream.

Because of this we didn't have to go before the judge. You see, there is a process and procedure you have to go through when you take a complaint before a judge, and there are certain things that have to happen, especially when you are going against Christian brothers and sisters. Isn't it better if we mediate together? I've realized that it is, for then it is a win-win situation.

I have learned a lot from this experience. In fact, after the mediation in the dream, I received a lot of favor with that particular book. Something started to happen, and I know it specifically has been an answer to prayer and because of that supernatural encounter with the angel.

PROTOCOLS OF HEAVEN

By Doug Addison

WHEN I WAS in South Africa, three angels were assigned to me, and all three returned home to the United States with me. I call that TWA—travel with angels! The angels are called Love, Fire, and Revelation.

After I got home, I immediately noticed that in meetings where I spoke, they would come as soon as I began to speak. I especially noticed that when I talked about them, their presence would come, and they came for the purpose of releasing what they carried.

In one of my first meetings after returning from South Africa, I noticed that the angel Love came into the room. I knew it because a thick blanket of God's presence, peace, and love came strongly on the people.

This happened right before lunchtime, and when I dismissed the meeting for the lunch break, no one moved. Now you know that when a group of Christians don't move for a lunch break, there must be a powerful presence of the Holy Spirit and angels!

The angel Revelation came too. And here is the amazing thing: when Revelation comes, I don't have to prophesy, and no one has to lay hands on the people. When Revelation comes into the room, people just start to receive revelation. People can leave the meeting without having been prayed for, and they receive it.

The angel Fire comes only once in a while, but when it does, the power is very strong for healing. People often fall under the power of God without anyone being near them and with no one praying over them.

But when I go to other churches where I'm not allowed to talk about angels, I still see Love, Fire, and Revelation there with me, but they are handcuffed because of the belief, or unbelief, really, of the people who will not let angels minister.

At other meetings I see these angels who have a specific purpose for ministry, and they are ready to release what they have brought. But when the leadership takes the meeting in a different direction, the level and presence those angels bring go way down, and they have to stand off to the side; they are prevented from ministering.

I have also begun to recognize that some churches have resident angels. You can see this through a specific type or style of ministry that a particular church does regularly. For example, some churches are strong worshipping churches and have resident worship angels. At other churches inner healing always seems to happen at ministry time, and that is because they have resident angels who work for inner healing. Then there are angels for evangelism or outreach to the poor. Often those ministries are associated with the angels at that church.

But when I come in to a church to minister, I am bringing something from the outside. The way I minister is more outside the box, so to speak. But I've noticed that the angels who come with me actually get permission from the resident angels first before they will operate in or minister what they bring. However, if the church leadership or anyone else in the church begins to minister with the angels they are used to operating with, then the angels I bring lose power. That happens because of the protocol of heaven. When it is operating, the leadership of the church establishes the spiritual authority and tone.

I like to have some fun with this, though.

I was invited once to speak at a church in another country, and the leadership had seen my blog, which describes different angelic encounters. They told me they did not want me to talk about angels.

Well, OK, but I do comedy. That's my ministry style. In fact, the Lord has told me to always just be myself. In the past when I have tried to minister like "regular" preachers, the power I carry tapers way off, so I have been released to be myself and do stand-up comedy as the way I minister. With who I am and with my style, well, it's hard to censor angels out. So when it comes to angels, I "let it slip out," let's just say.

I'll say, "I'd like to talk about ministering with angels, but there's not really time to talk about it because I'm not allowed to, so I won't bring up ministering with angels." Comedy is fun. Ministering with angels is too.

Here's an example of what can happen when angels are given permission to work freely. I was ministering once at an arena event with more than one thousand people in attendance. The event was being filmed, but an everyday secular media team was doing the filming. Well, the power of God came so strong as the angels and Holy Spirit were released to minister that the secular camera guys fell from their camera chairs. They were glued to the floor and could not get up.

Later, the head of the media crew came up to me and told me that he had filmed everything from The Rolling Stones to the pope, but he had never seen anything like what he saw in our meeting. He'd never seen his camera guys fall out of their chairs and not be able to get up from the floor! That was the most powerful time I think I've ever seen when angels were given permission to minister.

THE TRAVEL AGENT ANGEL

By Doug Addison

Sometimes angels come in glory, but sometimes they come cloaked as a person. When that happens, we don't always realize we are in the presence of an angel.

In 1993 I went with a group of people to Seoul, South Korea, to study the effects of church growth and church prayer. Some of the largest churches in the world were in South Korea then. There were about twenty of us in this group.

We didn't go as a tour group or as an official group of any kind. We went over on our own. So when we arrived in Seoul, there wasn't anyone to pick us up or organize anything for us. We just flew in, and there we were.

Well, pretty quickly there was a lot of confusion. Twenty of us from the San Francisco Bay area all arrived to find ourselves totally lost. There we were, with all our luggage, overwhelmed with the area. Frankly, most of us were almost in tears. We didn't know where to go or how to get there.

Fortunately a Korean travel agent named Sue, who spoke perfect English, summoned us. She came over and started waving for all of us to get on the bus that was waiting for us. It was air-conditioned, and she brought each of us water, which was great because we all were parched. She rode with us as far as the bus could go, then she told us the bus wouldn't be going farther because the local streets were too narrow.

So she got us all off the bus, got all of our luggage, and hailed five or six taxis for us. She handed each of us notes written in Korean for the cab drivers so they would know where to take us. And off we went.

The next day we told the people we were staying with, "Hey, thanks. That was cool to send the travel agent and the bus for us." But no one had done that. No one had organized anything for us.

A few days later we all were back in the middle of Seoul, a city of more than nine million people at that time, and we were completely lost again. Some people in our group had gotten separated from us, and we didn't know where to go or what we were doing. Our travel agent, Sue, was there again to get us back together and help us.

On the last day we were visiting a folk center way outside of town. The pastor who was with us was a diabetic. He had gotten separated from the group and became very sick. He actually started going into diabetic shock and losing his sight.

But he started to come out of the shock and come to, and when he did, he looked up and Sue was suddenly there. She told him, "Your group is over there. They are over there." Then she kind of pushed him over toward us, and we found him and were able to help him. Sue, however, just went away.

Everyone in that group is convinced to this day that Sue was an angel, cloaked in clothing as a person. She was there to save our lives.

THE ANGEL OF THE CITY

By Michael Maiden

WHEN I WAS in Kampala, Uganda, I spoke at the Parliament building to more than five thousand pastors. I shared with them about the angel of their city and how God assigns angels to territories, even nations. For instance, the archangel Michael is the angel assigned to the nation of Israel.

Angels have assignments, they have jurisdictions, and they have delegated responsibilities. They operate in orderly fashion, just like any government. God has order, then layers of authority, and He sends angels to war and to work for His will.

In this beautiful Parliament building the ceiling was probably eighty feet high. I was on the stage, and next to me were some of the leaders, staff, and evangelists from the city's churches, including Pastor Phil Pringle from Sydney, Australia. We were leading this conference for pastors from across the continent of Africa.

As I talked about the angel of the city, I watched as four or five gentlemen on the stage with me suddenly turn their eyes from me and stare at the ceiling. All five at once did this. I thought, "Oh, they're just bored. Ha!"

But after the service all of them ran up to me and told me they all had shared a common vision simultaneously. Each one had seen the very same thing at the same time.

"As you were describing the angel of the city," they said, "we saw a huge being walk through the room. He was so tall that we could see only up to about his chest. He was dressed in a white garment, and with one step he walked through this five-thousand-seat auditorium. He just passed through it like that! One step!"

They couldn't get over the angelic manifestation.

At the very moment I was speaking about angels, those men had witnessed a powerful manifestation of an angelic being—just stepping through the building in a simple yet powerful way.

35

Through it they were made aware of the genuineness of the message.

I didn't see the angel, but I did see the reaction of the five people who had a common, open vision of an angelic visitation.

Michael Maiden and his wife, Mary, lead Church for the Nations (www.cftn.com) in Phoenix, Arizona. He also serves on the apostolic board of Church on the Rock International, a dynamic ministry that oversees more than six thousand churches worldwide. He is the author of seven books, including The Joshua Generation *and* 8 Simple Rules for a Blessed Life. *Maiden holds both master's and doctoral degrees in Christian psychology.*

A SEASON OF ANGELIC
VISITATION

By Michael Maiden

T HE BIBLE SAYS angels are servants, that they are sent to serve us (Heb. 1:14). But our chief relationship with them is indirect, not direct, because our relationship is with God.

The Bible says in Psalm 103 that the angels hearken to the voice of His word. So when I speak God's Word, when it's anointed and the will of God—whether as a prophetic word or by quoting the written Word in a revelatory moment—an angel hears it as if God said it and responds to it to carry out an order.

The angels hear it and respond because they can't tell the difference between my voice and God's voice when His Word is in both. It's a beautiful relationship.

When angels appeared in the Bible, the people often would ask, "What's your name?" The angels would often reply, "I can't tell you my name."

Angels are forbidden from revealing too much about themselves because any attention on them is attention diverted from God. It is Luciferic. It is sinful, prideful. So the angels would say, "That's not important," when asked their name.

Getting to know an angel's name is a form of one-on-one intimacy with angels, which is forbidden because an angel's job is to point people to God. Any real angelic visitation, if it's as a revelatory moment or encounter, is always going to be God-filled because that's their only occupation, that's their primary passion, and they're very singularly and purely focused on that.

A great preacher, Kenneth E. Hagin, said that an angel appeared to him and gave him spectacular visions and said some spectacular things to him. And Hagin said to the angel, "I won't believe any of this unless you show me where it is in the Word." And the angel was not upset about that because it's a very good guideline.

An angelic visitation will never supersede or exceed any revelatory truth of the Bible. That's the safety zone we have.

We are currently in the greatest time of angelic visitations since the birth of Christ. Three times in history angels have had a heightened visitation. First, at Creation, we are told that the sons of God sang (Job 38:6–8). This is a reference to an angelic choir singing at Creation—a symphony, a romantic moment as God gives birth to the universe—time, space, and matter.

Second, at the birth of Christ the heavens were torn open and the shepherds heard an angelic choir praising God and saying, "Glory to God in the highest" (Luke 2:13–15).

The third is now, in the last days. We are in a heightened season of angelic manifestation just like those earlier pivotal, historic moments—the creation of the world, the first coming of Christ, and the second coming of Christ.

This is a wonderful time because the more the enemy escalates his evil and his demonic activity, the more angelic activity there is. Evil will always be exceeded by a heavenly presence and angelic visitations. So where sin abounds, grace much more abounds!

The angels are being released. It's a very exciting time in history. We are going to see a wave of miraculous angelic activities. Whether or not we fully discern all the angelic stuff is not important to the angel, as long as we know God did something.

GO GET THE ANGELS

By David Herzog

THERE ARE DIFFERENT kinds of angels: territorial angels, worship angels, warring angels, financial angels, and others.

We have seen major miracles of finances when financial angels were involved. There is also a treasury in heaven. Just as the US government has a treasury, so heaven has a treasury and an angel who works as the treasurer of heaven.

You can work with these angels of heaven to bring heaven to earth. What does that look like? Well, we know how it is in heaven—it's pretty good! There are healing and salvation in heaven, so there are angels to bring healing and salvation. There are angels to set up divine appointments for you. Angels will put people right in your path who are ready for salvation. It's pretty fun.

As for the territorial angels, what's interesting to me is that pastors and Christians can tell me all about the demons over their cities. They have maps and grids and can point to the streets where the demons are. But when I ask, "What are the territorial angels over your city?" they can't name even one.

I tell them even if they were to free the entire city of demons, they still would have to invite the corresponding angels to fill the places the demons occupied. Satan has copied the government of heaven, so the ruling structure for every demon on earth—the principalities, powers, governments, and so on—has been copied from the angelic structure. That's why if you find out what the original angelic structure was in a location, you can displace the demonic much easier.

I see this all the time when I go into a new place and the people say, "Our town is so hard; nothing happens here," but when we show up, miracles, signs, and wonders take place.

This happened in Portland, Maine, which is a very New Age area, a very hard area in America. But for us it was flowing like honey—angels, the glory of God, the healing power of God. It happens this way for us because I always ask when we get to a city, "What is the territorial angel assigned to this city?"

Most people know about territorial spirits, but they know about the demonic not the angelic. If you bring the angel who is supposed to be ruling that city and unleash him, things will happen! It is more effective than finding a tree or a monument and screaming at the concrete for three hours the way some people do to drive out demonic forces. Why not bring the ruling angel with you? That's fun! It is exciting!

And it is easy to do—just get into the glory realm of God.

Sometimes when I am in a new city I do not feel the angelic authority that is meant to be there, so I'll go get it. Does that make sense? I will go into the glory realm and get it.

I close my eyes, and I go into the heavenly realm. I go to the throne of God, and I worship the Father. I ask Him for some angels, and then I come back down. It is just like you're soaking and worshipping in God's presence, but you come back down with an entourage of angels.

Getting into the glory is the secret to my whole ministry. I get in the glory, and when Jesus the King of glory is there, He has an entourage of angels with Him.

All you have to do is get into the glory, and you automatically have the angels.

Once in a while when I am in a tough place spiritually, I will go into the heavenly realm and see myself at the throne, and when I come back down, it is as if the enemy gets clobbered. I do this instead of doing what some people do—going one on one directly against one demonic presence at a time.

For example, when they are aware of a demon attacking them, they bind it in Jesus's name. It's like hand-to-hand combat. But if that's not enough, then you have to go over the demon's head. You have to go into the heavenly realm and seek your place in the Most High. Then, when you come back down, the enemy doesn't see the blow coming. *Whoosh!* It goes right over his head and suddenly, whack!

I was in a meeting once, and religious spirits were there. I lay on the floor during the worship time and went completely into the glory realm. When I heard my name as they were calling me to the microphone to preach, I came back. But the experience opened up a whole realm for me.

I always think of Elijah and his servant who, in the natural, could see only that they were outnumbered by enemy soldiers. But Elijah prayed, "LORD, I pray, open his eyes that he may see" in the angelic realm (2 Kings 6:16–18). Elijah knew if his servant could see into the angelic realm the way he could, then his servant would know there were more angels with them than enemies against them.

This is the kind of work I do with angels all the time.

David Herzog and his wife, Stephanie, are the founders of David Herzog Ministries and authors of numerous books on the glory, health, and relationships. The hosts of the weekly TV program The Glory Zone (www.TheGloryZone.org), they have ministered in crusades, conferences, revivals, and outreaches in the United States, Canada, Western and Eastern Europe, Africa, Russia, Australia, New Zealand, Argentina, Peru, Brazil, Mexico, Guatemala, Korea, Malaysia, Indonesia, Singapore, Papua New Guinea, the Caribbean, the Arctic, Kuwait, Dubai, Qatar, Bahrain, Sri Lanka, Madagascar, Vanuatu, and Israel. After living overseas for twelve years, the Herzogs now live in Sedona, Arizona.

ANGELS INCREASING FINANCES

By David Herzog

I HAVE HAD TWO significant experiences in which the presence of angels shifted financial situations.

One was during a crusade in we did in Paris, France. Doing a crusade in the city is unheard of. It is very hard to organize. But we rented a big building, and God packed it out with people. There were miracles, healings, signs, and wonders. During the meetings I asked the Lord, "What are we to do about paying for this place?" Not enough money had come in through the offerings to pay for the building rental.

So I told the people who collected the offerings to count the money. They did and reported the amount. It wasn't enough. But there was such an angelic presence in that place. So I told them, "Count the money again." They said they would, but that they were confident the first count was right.

When they counted the money again, the amount doubled. So I told them to count it again. It tripled. I told them to count it again, and it quadrupled; and that was enough to pay for the crusade building. It was the result of angels working in the area of supernatural provision.

Another time we were in the jungle in a place called Maripasoula. It is in French Guiana where the capital is Cayenne.

We took a seaplane deep into the jungle, into a truly primitive area, where there was a huge tree so contorted I'd never seen anything like it. It looked haunted. I asked the pastor I was with, "What is that?" He told me it was a demonic tree. It was where the native people worshipped—they would worship the tree and channel demons that used the tree like an antenna.

"That is so strange!" I said.

But the pastor told me, "Do not talk against that tree. If you do, they will kill you."

I wondered what I should do. So I preached on the cross—the only tree that can bring salvation! Since these people worshipped the contorted tree for protection, health, prosperity, and whatever else, I preached that there is a greater tree: the cross.

As I preached, the power of God came, and the angels came and the glory came. Then, in the middle of the meeting, the Lord told me to have the people give an offering. I questioned that because these were very poor people. I told the Lord I had come there to help them and that they didn't have anything to give. They didn't even have shoes—nothing.

But the Lord told me, "Take up an offering. Have them give. You do not understand; giving is worship. These people are worshipping the demonic entities and giving them food and gold and all sorts of things. If you have them give now, it will shift their worship. It will bring down My glory and the angels because worship opens the heavens—just like when Elijah put the sacrifice on the altar."

So I did. I took up an offering, knowing that one-fourth of the room was witches and sorcerers.

And the people gave. And when they started giving, mass deliverance began to occur. Suddenly, during the actual offering, healings, signs, and wonders broke out. It was amazing.

One-fourth of the town was saved at that service.

Afterward the pastor and I went back to my cabin. There are no hotels in this jungle town because it is totally primitive. In the cabin I saw an angel standing behind the pastor. As I looked at the angel, it started talking to me, and I started prophesying over the pastor and telling him what would happen in his ministry over the next five years.

Then he looked at me and saw an angel at my back. I could feel the heat, and the pastor started telling me what was going to happen in *my* ministry and in *my* life over the next five years.

As we were doing this, the glory got so thick that we went to the floor, calling out, "Lord, we worship You!" The glory was so strong that we couldn't move. I wasn't even sure my body could physically handle it, which I never thought I would say. But the pastor said to me, "Let's move out of here." So we crawled out and went into the kitchen area. We turned the lights on and had some water. But then all the angels followed us into the kitchen, and more angels came, and we were calling out again, "We worship You, Lord!" The angels were helping us to worship Jesus.

It was such a thick glory that we decided to crawl back into the room we'd come from, and when we did we heard the chickens and other animals outside going nuts. It sounded like they were getting deliverance! Something was going on that neither the pastor nor I had ever seen happen. When the glory came in our room, the demonic in the area around it went berserk. It was amazing.

What else was amazing is, after that night, after taking the offering in the midst of the angelic and the glory, money has been pouring in from all over the place into that village, the pastor told us. Before we came, they had nothing—no money, nothing. Now they have exploded financially.

People from everywhere are simply compelled to bless them and help them. An angel represents God's provision for that ministry so the believers there can win the whole town. It is really exciting.

Now wherever we go, I tell people, "If you are bored with your Christian life, you need to connect to the glory and work with the angels."

THE GOVERNMENTAL ANGEL

By David Herzog

I HAVE A GOVERNMENTAL angel who travels often with me. Once when this angel was with me, I was flying from Paris to Washington DC to preach at several churches in a period of five days.

During the flight the heavy glory fell, and the angelic presence was strong. God said to me in that moment, "Declare right now that before you leave, you will be in the White House to pray."

"What?" I responded.

But the Lord insisted.

"Say it now while My glory is on you. Do not miss the moment because the angels will go ahead of you and open the door."

So I said, "I will be in the White House before I leave in the next couple of days, in Jesus's name."

And when I declared it, it released the angels to do it.

When I landed, a pastor picked me up and said, "Let's drive in front of the White House. Have you ever seen it?"

I knew it was a clue, so as we drove along in front of the presidential residence, I looked at it and said under my breath, "White House, open up."

I preached for the next couple of days and really forgot about the whole White House thing until the last day of our meetings, when a woman came to me on Sunday and told me, "I am an intercessor. God has told me you need to go into the White House to pray."

"Who are you?" I asked. "How did you know that?"

"Don't worry about that," she said. "I know people. Give me your social security number and I will get you in. It might take a few weeks."

"I don't have a few weeks," I told her. "I live overseas, and I am leaving in two days."

Her response was, "That'll be tough, but let's see what happens.

I have friends who work next to the White House and maybe they can get you in."

So I gave her my social security number, and the very next day she called me saying, "This is amazing! We've never seen this! You have been cleared by the FBI and CIA to go into the White House with a worker to take you on a private tour!"

I was given a private tour of the East Wing and many other places. The angels had opened it up supernaturally. It was totally angelic.

I've seen this kind of pattern repeated, in which the Lord instructs me to go to places and tells me to prophesy it, and then angels open it up for me.

For instance, when I was going to New York City, God told me, "Go to the United Nations and prophesy." Not knowing how to get into the United Nations, I just did what I knew to do: I got into the presence of God and in the atmosphere of the glory I declared, "United Nations, open up!"

When I do that, I know an angel is released to open the door for me. I then remembered a woman I had met years earlier who had told me if I ever wanted to visit the United Nations I should call her.

I called her and said, "I'm flying in to New York City from Dubai. I'll arrive on Wednesday."

She said, "That's funny, that's the only day you can get in."

She arranged it for me, and I was able to go in and hold a meeting with some of the UN workers and to prophesy. I found myself prophesying against "dividing the line of Israel."

Little did I know that at the exact moment I was there in the United Nations prophesying, a secret meeting was being held upstairs from where we were for the purpose of trying to divide the boundary of Israel and preempt other things from happening. But I was decreeing, "Don't do this." So I know something was happening in the spirit.

These governmental angels have been opening things up like crazy. They open fascinating doors in government.

When I was in Moscow, a door opened there. I was in Vanuatu, a South Pacific island, with my wife, and we had the opportunity to pray for the president to be healed. We also ministered to the prime minister, and he came to the crusade and was running around in the meeting.

This is because angels are opening these doors for us supernaturally.

Angels are fun! They are awesome and exciting! We do not worship them, of course. But some Christians are so scared to approach them. They are scared they might sin by interacting with them or that they might start worshipping them. These things cause people to ignore angels.

I would say, ask the Lord and work with your angels. Ask the Lord to show you who your angels are.

IN THE COURTS OF HEAVEN

By David Herzog

O NE DAY I was praying, and I went to heaven. Now I know that sounds funny to say, but that's what happened. I closed my eyes and saw I was in heaven.

I was walking around, I was in the throne room worshipping God, and to the right of the throne room was the Crystal Sea. I went there. It was nice. You can actually swim in it, and it feels really nice.

Then I went to a place called the Courts of Heaven. In there it's a whole different realm. If you go to heaven and don't know where the courts are, you can ask for directions and someone will lead you there. It's like a courtroom and there is a judge—God the Father, but sitting as judge. It is really amazing.

One of the types of matters dealt with in the court is when someone takes advantage of you and steals from you. Whether you have been ripped off in business or in a ministry deal, you can go to the Courts of Heaven.

I have learned that often when this sort of thing happens to us, we do go to God with it. We are angry about it, and we forgive the person, which brings some closure, but we do not get our stuff back. We don't get what was stolen from us.

The Word tells us that we not only are supposed to get it back but also to be repaid seven times. The reason we are not getting back what was stolen and being repaid seven times is we are not going to the Courts of Heaven.

We know how to go to the Father to have a heart wound healed, and we know that we have to forgive. But we never get the justice aspect unless we come to the Father as a judge also.

When the Father told me that, my instant reaction was, "Oh, my gosh, I did not realize that!" But it suddenly was obvious. We go to the Father as our healer when we need healing. In the same way we need to go to the Father as our judge for justice.

I wanted to go to the Courts of Heaven for justice because I had been ripped off. It was a really large amount of money, and it had happened overseas in another country. Before going inside, I cleansed myself with the blood of Jesus, covering anything I knew that needed to be cleansed. I said, "Lord, I forgive them."

Then I was counseled on how to bring the matter properly before the court.

I was told, "You talk to Me like I am your Father at the dinner table, and that's good; but imagine that you are talking to your father one night at dinner and telling him about the injustice done to you. He understands, but your father also happens to be the judge of that town. So he tells you, 'Son, bring this before me in the court tomorrow, where I can hear the case officially in my authority as judge and then do something about it.'"

He continued. "Bring this matter to Me. I care more about this than you do."

So I did just that.

Before I got inside the courtroom, I suddenly realized why I had to repent of any bad attitudes—because the accuser of the brethren was there too.

It was like a DMZ, like the demilitarized zone between North Korea and South Korea. It is a place where the enemy can be, and he was. He was saying all sorts of things to me, such as, "You don't deserve justice. Look at your reaction."

But the judge said, "No, that evidence is not permissible in this court because he already brought it as evidence."

From this I was learning the protocols of how it works in heaven: you repent before you go in, and then the enemy cannot use anything against you that you have already repented of. I had repented of my bad attitudes, and I had forgiven the people who stole from me. So in this court the enemy couldn't hold my bad attitude against me as a reason to disqualify me from justice.

Then the Lord said to me, "I declare justice over you and recompense."

Amazingly within forty-eight hours the businesspeople who had ripped me off wired all the money back into my account.

Approximately $86,000! These men initially had the consensus that they were not giving me the money because, in their opinion, it wasn't mine. But after my trip to the Courts of Heaven, they had an emergency meeting and suddenly sent it all back to me.

I know that some major angels were involved because when God releases stuff, He does it through angels. The protocol is that we ask the Father in the name of Jesus, through the Holy Spirit who is on the earth. Under the Holy Spirit is the angelic authority.

So we pray and go to the Father in the name of Jesus. Then the Holy Spirit, who is on the earth, uses angels. That's what is happening in the spirit.

You may find yourself calling out only the name of Jesus, for example, if you are in a car accident. You may just say "Jesus!" but then all these other things take place. You just find yourself in the middle of a situation where angels suddenly are released.

You might not have known or actually gone through all the steps, but the power is in the name of Jesus, and that's what is going on behind the scenes.

The justice of God issued in the Courts of Heaven is really awesome.

Another time that I was in heaven, I was looking at Jesus face-to-face. He looked at me and said, "You are in Bethel, Israel." In the natural I was not in Israel. I was in the heavenly realm with Jesus, but I was there in Bethel at a gate of heaven.

Jesus said to me, "Thank you for touching Isaac." I knew what He meant by that because my team and I had been sharing the gospel with Jewish people who were getting saved.

Then Jesus continued, "But now go to Ishmael. Organize a conference for me in Jerusalem." I said OK, but I didn't understand what He was asking of me.

Two days later I was invited to organize a conference in Jerusalem. I agreed to because the Lord has just personally asked me to do it. Right after that conference I was invited to a lot of Muslim countries where I had never been before. Within weeks I was in Kuwait, Qatar, Bahrain, in Dubai four times, and in Indonesia. So many Muslims were being touched and getting saved and healed.

This is proof that when you go to the heavenly realm, the angels are completely connected with what happens there, and they bring it back to earth with you because they are the servants that open the doors for us. They minister to the heirs of salvation, the Bible says (Heb. 1:14).

The angels are purposed to help the heirs of salvation so that when God gives a word, it comes on earth in such a way that Jesus doesn't have to get off the throne to do it. The angels on the earth do it for you in Jesus's name. It's fun! Angels and heavenly stories are fun.

THE ANGEL OF HOLINESS

By Stephanie Herzog

W E WERE DOING open-air meetings on a mountaintop in
Sedona, Arizona, and the atmosphere of the glory was powerful! I had been preaching that day, and when I had finished, a little
boy came up to me. He wasn't looking at me, though; he was looking
high in the air. He said, "There are huge angels dressed in white that
stand right behind you when you preach."

You could tell that as he was saying this to me, he was actually
looking up at the huge angels. I have felt these angels often before
when I preach. They are holiness angels. They are always dressed
in white and accompany me to bring holiness into the atmosphere.

This is what happens when you minister from the glory; it's a
whole different thing. David, my husband, and I have been ministering like this since 1999, and it releases signs, wonders, and
miracles all the time. We often see healing miracles where people
actually—physically—get new body parts! I believe it is because the
angels get excited when we talk about the glory.

I have seen angels' wings *whoosh* around just because we talk about
the glory. When you add that to an atmosphere in which people are
ready and really believing for miracles, the angels get so excited that
they just start releasing the miracles—and the new body parts. It
is faith that pulls the miracles from the heavenly realm. The angels
disperse these body parts, and we see it actually manifest in the natural realm as a miracle.

This is what can happen when you partner and team with angels.

We see it in different ways when we travel to other countries
because we get to team with angels from these other countries who
are new to us. It's really awesome because you can see how your angels
interact with the new angels, and it affects how the people interact.

This is when we see great signs and wonders, such as the manifestation of gold dust and gemstones. I like to laugh and say that we get

all excited about the gold dust, but really it's just the angels dusting themselves off, dusting off their wings and clothes. In heaven the pavement is made of gold, so for the angels the gold is really just like dust. It's the same with the gemstones; we are all excited about these gemstones and how precious they are, but really the angels are just picking the pebbles out of their toes.

Stephanie Herzog and her husband, David, are the founders of David Herzog Ministries and the authors of numerous books on the glory, health, and relationships. The hosts of the weekly TV program The Glory Zone (www.TheGloryZone.org), they have ministered in crusades, conferences, revivals, and outreaches in the United States, Canada, Western and Eastern Europe, Africa, Russia, Australia, New Zealand, Argentina, Peru, Brazil, Mexico, Guatemala, Korea, Malaysia, Indonesia, Singapore, Papua New Guinea, the Caribbean, the Arctic, Kuwait, Dubai, Qatar, Bahrain, Sri Lanka, Madagascar, Vanuatu, and Israel. After living for twelve years overseas, the Herzogs now live in Sedona, Arizona.

THE AZUSA STREET ANGEL

By Rick Wright

W E NEED TO believe God and trust Him to send His angels. He sends them regardless, but He wants us to be in faith with Him, to be in fellowship with Him, and to believe the truth about His holy angels.

I have had several encounters, but two that meant a great deal to me happened here in Los Angeles, California. I was born and raised here and now pastor a church here, so the things that the Lord is doing here are very special to me.

A couple of years ago I went with some intercessors for a prayer walk, and we went up to the famous Hollywood sign. We were walking about a quarter mile below the sign, which is on a hillside.

As I stood looking up at the sign, I saw a star come slowly down and hover right over it. As this happened, several large, black birds suddenly flew off.

It made me think of Revelation 9:1, where the Bible describes angels as stars. And seeing this angel, this star, come down and chase off the blackness, the darkness—what I believe were evil spirits—was a real encouragement to me. It told me to always know that our angels are more powerful than any principalities and powers, whether they are over nations or cities. The angels of God come down, and the battle belongs to the Lord.

Another encounter I had was related to the Azusa Street Revival from the early 1900s. It happened while I was attending a meeting on Bonnie Brae Street, which is the original location of the revival that broke out and moved to Azusa Street.

After I arrived for the meeting and started to walk in through the back door, I was told to take my shoes off. When I did, I came under the power of the Spirit of God, the presence of God, and I couldn't really even talk. I was overwhelmed. I went into the meeting to sit down and pray with the group of intercessors I was with. But

I couldn't even communicate with them. I knew I was having an encounter with an angel.

So I left that meeting room and went into the next room. I was experiencing very strong impressions, and I was unable to function. By that I mean that I was so overwhelmed by the presence and power of God I could not be a part of the prayer meeting.

I sat by myself, overwhelmed by the presence of God through this angel. A really wonderful elder came in to sit with me, and I said to him, "I am being overwhelmed. There is an angel here that is telling me he is the angel from Azusa Street, that his name is Historic and that he creates history."

After several hours the group I was with was ready to leave the prayer meeting, and we left together. I apologized to them for not being a part of the meeting and tried to explain how I was overwhelmed. I was unable to explain what was going on. I said, "I'm having some kind of an angelic encounter. I'm overwhelmed."

The next day the same angel came to me and began to speak to me about the plans and promises for Los Angeles and for California.

Angels have an important function in the moves of God. They open the gates. As intercessors, many times we think that we are the ones doing it, but to be honest with you, it is these angels who see and live in the Spirit. They've been with God forever, for eons of time, and they are the ones opening the gates.

They are the ones the Lord sends first. We see this in the Bible at the birth of our Lord when the angels came first to announce His plan. We also see this when the angels went ahead of Israel into the Promised Land (Exod. 23:20). We see it with Abraham. When he wanted a wife for his son, he sent his servant out on behalf of his son and told the servant, "My angel will go with you." (See Genesis 24.)

Angels are very important in their role of going ahead of us. They know the Lord. They know His purposes. They can see demons. They have the whole plan—and, believe me, they are doing much more than intercessors and even prophetic intercessors sometimes realize.

I thank God for the angels of the Lord! Thank You, Lord Jesus, for being the Lord of Hosts and for releasing angels on our behalf!

Angels are commissioned by Jesus—He is the head of the whole thing.

I am so thankful, Lord, for Your wonderful, glorious angels. Amen.

Rick Wright and his wife, Pam, are the founders and senior pastors of The Gathering Place (www.GatheringPlace.us) in North Hollywood, California, a church plant of Harvest Rock Church in Pasadena, California.

PART 2

ANGELIC MESSENGERS

Then, being divinely warned in a dream that they
should not return to Herod, they departed for their
own country another way. Now when they had
departed, behold, an angel of the Lord appeared
to Joseph in a dream, saying, "Arise, take the young
Child and His mother, flee to Egypt, and stay there
until I bring you word; for Herod will seek the
young Child to destroy Him."
—Matthew 2:12–13

CATCH!

By Joshua Mills

SEVERAL YEARS AGO I was ministering in Victoria, British Columbia. After one of the meetings, when I normally would move into altar ministry, I felt like I was supposed to go back to my hotel and release the ministry team at the church to take over the altar and healing ministries.

So the altar team came forward to begin ministering, and healing was released. I told the pastor I was ready to go to my hotel. I felt such an urgency to get back.

When I arrived and opened my hotel room door, the lights were still off inside, but I could see two feet on the other side of the room—there was a man standing across from me.

At first I was fearful because I thought someone had gotten into my room, and there I was, all by myself. But those thoughts came and went very quickly. The man standing in my room was an angel, and before I could walk into the room, he said, "Catch!" He took this huge fireball—it lit up the entire room—and threw it. He threw the fireball right at me as I was standing in the doorway about to enter the room.

I reached out to catch it, and when I did, it exploded into gold dust all over the frame of the door. Gold dust was everywhere! It was on the ceiling, on the walls, on the carpet, and all over my face. It had exploded everywhere.

Then the angel said, "Get ready to catch. More miracles are coming."

And at that he was gone.

I was trembling, completely. I had earthquakes on the inside. I had butterflies inside. I was shaking and didn't know what to say or do. I went into the room and just began praying to God. I said, "God, show me what that is all about. Give me an understanding of this."

And then for more than three hours I stayed in that place of awe. I was in awe of the glory of God, in awe of how awesome His presence is, in awe of how much He wants to do for us, but we are unaware of it.

Finally I called my wife, Janet Angela. It took that long before I was able to call her. I tried to describe what had happened to me. The next morning I spoke with the pastor and his wife about it. We all were amazed by it. I don't think they fully understood the awesomeness of it, but they were amazed, and I told them, "God is doing something really good."

I know this: the reason God sends the angelic realm to the earth for interaction with mankind is so His purposes, the purposes of heaven, can be released on the earth and so Jesus Christ will be glorified. That is the reason God allows these angelic interactions with mankind.

And so I knew God was preparing to do something great—and in a new way; He was preparing a new way to release the gospel message about Jesus Christ with power.

The next night as I preached at the church meeting, I was really excited about what God was doing. As I ministered in the glory, I looked up from the pulpit, and suddenly the same angel who was in my room the night before was standing right at the very back of the church.

I thought, "Oh, God, not right here!" That's because anybody who knows me knows that my reflexes are really bad. If I were to go out and play sports, I probably would be the last one picked for a team, especially to be a catcher. But you know, God has a sense of humor. The Bible says He sits in the heavens and laughs (Ps. 2:4). In my case He sent the angel to the meeting, and the angel started pulling out another fireball. I knew what was coming.

"Catch!" he said as he threw the ball of fire.

He was standing all the way at the back of the sanctuary. He threw it over the heads of the people, but instead of throwing it directly to me at the podium, he threw it so it came just over the head of a woman sitting on the left side of the room. I had to run to catch it!

Of course when God tells you to do something—when an angel comes with a message—you need to do what God is saying to do. As I reached to catch the ball of fire, it exploded into gold dust all over her. Gold dust exploded in the natural over her face, her head, her shoulders, even all over the people on the row in front of her and behind her.

People have asked me whether anyone else was able to see the angel. Several people said they saw the angel in the back of the room; several others said they saw the fireball flying through the air. But I tell you this, every person in that room saw the manifestation of the gold dust when it exploded! They saw it explode in the air and then come down.

There was a word of knowledge inside the fireball—a revelation from God came with it—and I began to get words of knowledge and to release them. The specific word that came was for the woman over whom the ball exploded. It was a word about finances for her. I declared the word of knowledge, but little did I know this woman was in need of a financial miracle. She was down to very little in her bank account, very little, and she needed a financial miracle. I didn't know, but God knew.

After I spoke that word of knowledge, the angel proceeded to pull out another fireball and said, "Catch!" Again, instead of throwing it to me where I was, he threw it to the opposite side of the sanctuary. I had to run all the way to the other side to catch it!

Again, when I caught it, words of knowledge began flowing. And once again, several people saw the angel and several others saw the fireball flying through the air. But when it exploded into the physical manifestation of gold dust, everyone in the place went nuts!

The people were so touched by the glory that night. There were so many miracles. The pastors compiled a list of more than forty miracles that occurred that night alone. Instant miracles happened—people received financial, healing, and deliverance miracles. There were so many different miracles that came forth, and the testimonies just continued to multiply in the days that followed.

Now going back to where this all began—in the hotel room—there is another amazing story about that.

What I didn't know was that in the very room where I stayed
witches had once stayed and performed witchcraft. The hotel staff
knew this because things had never been the same since the witches
were there. The plumbing broke constantly. No matter how often
they fixed it, no matter what they did, the plumbing would constantly break. The electrical system was the same way. It broke down
constantly.

There also was a mark the witches put on either the ceiling or
the wall—some kind of a satanic symbol. It wouldn't go away. Hotel
maintenance painted over it, again and again, but it always came
back through the paint.

Well, the night God released His glory through the angel in my
room, everything changed. Suddenly the plumbing and electrical
systems worked properly again without anyone having to do anything. The satanic symbol supernaturally disappeared.

When the owner of the hotel learned about the angelic fireball
encounter and how it had eliminated the problems in the hotel, he
was overwhelmed. He was overwhelmed that God would do this in
his hotel, that God would cause this divine appointment for me to
stay in the very room where the witchcraft had been practiced. He
was overwhelmed by how God, so suddenly, cleared the whole place
out with His glory.

Since then the owner has entered a new realm of blessing and
financial prosperity. The release of God's glory has even opened
doors of favor for the pastor and his wife on the whole of Victoria
Island. The hotelier owns the most hotels in Victoria, and he
arranged with the pastor and his wife to give them, free of charge,
as many rooms for as many guest speakers as they want to bring in.

Why has there been such a release of supernatural favor? Why
has there been an overflow of blessing as a result of this angelic
encounter? Because the glory realm was released, and in that glory
realm the angelic was released, and with the angelic came miracles
because the glory realm is the presence of God—and where His
glory is there is the fullness of His presence.

Joshua Mills is an anointed minister, recording artist, conference speaker, and author of more than six hundred songs. Joshua and his wife, Janet Angela, minister worldwide through their ministry, New Wine International (www.NewWineRevival.org), carrying the message that "praise changes the atmosphere." Their services are often marked by signs, wonders, supernatural encounters, and creative miracles. The couple lives in British Columbia, Canada, with their two children.

ANGEL SPIES

By Katie Souza

I AM A REAL seeker of answers from God. My attitude is always, "God, just tell me what to do, and I will do it!" So when I have a problem or am in a difficult situation, I just tell Him, "Give me the path, the strategy; tell me how to do it step by step, and I will take care of it."

That has been my continual cry for years, and God always answers me. As I started getting into more complicated situations, I needed more complicated answers.

I remember one night when God was speaking to me, He said, "I want you to call forth 'the spies.'" I didn't understand that at all. Spies? What is that? So I asked Him to explain what He meant.

I went to an online Bible study program and typed in "spies." It brought up Numbers 21, the account of when the Israelites as a nation actually entered the Promised Land to occupy it. They did so via the route of Atharim (v. 1). This is the route the twelve spies of Israel had previously taken when they went into the land to spy it out and see if it was good.

Years later when Israel finally entered the Promised Land, they found this same path the spies had taken. It was the route that led them in to possess the land. The Israelites knew how to return into the Promised Land because the spies had already been there.

As I read that scripture, the Lord told me "the spies" He told me to call forth are an actual angelic force. When you call for them, you release them to go before you, to find the route, which is the specific way you need to go to get to your promised land. They go ahead of you and come back to release the directions to you. They may say, "Go right here," "Go left here," "Go up here," or "Go down there." That is their job. They are the spies who give you the directions, the way to get into your promised land.

At different times since this discovery and understanding, the

Lord has told me to "Call forth the spies!" I call them and release these angelic spies. In a matter of weeks I begin to get revelation and answers to a problem. Then I am able to take hold of the answer, which takes me in and gives me entry into a new area of my promised land.

A specific example of this is once when I needed a really big miracle, a big breakthrough. I needed specific directions on how to get into an area of my promised land. So I prayed, and I released the spies.

Then one night I was in my kitchen at home, not doing anything spiritual mind you; I was just making a peanut butter and banana sandwich. I wasn't even praying or thinking much about my situation or even thinking about God. But suddenly the spies appeared in my kitchen. I could actually see them.

These angel spies were right there in front of me. They all wore safari outfits, as if they had been on a safari. They wore hats on their heads and carried guns, binoculars, maps, and everything else you would need if you were going on a journey to chart a way. They talked amongst themselves as I just sat there watching them in total amazement. I could see them with my eyes open, and even though they were very obvious to me and very easy to see, they were transparent, not solid. I could see them and see through them at the same time. They stood there for a moment, talking and doing things amongst themselves, and then, just like that, they disappeared.

The next day I began to get a major revelation for a huge breakthrough I had been waiting on for a long time. In fact, since that moment in my kitchen, I have seen countless miracles occur through the strategies released when the angel spies show up.

A former felon, Katie Souza is now an author and speaker, and the founder of Expected End Ministries (www.ExpectedEndMinistries .com) based in Maricopa, Arizona. Through her ministry thousands of people have been taught how to operate in the supernatural realm, experienced physical and emotional healing, and have been equipped to fulfill their God-given destinies.

ARE YOU READY?

By Darren Wilson

I HAVE PRODUCED, DIRECTED, and released three documentaries on the supernatural, *The Finger of God, Furious Love,* and *Father of Lights.*

I didn't begin as a fan or a believer in the supernatural. It really began because I *didn't* believe. In fact, it began in May 2006 when I went to that crazy church up in Toronto, the Toronto Airport Christian Fellowship (now called Catch the Fire). I didn't want to go, but my wife conned me into it. I hated every minute of it.

There was some big conference, and there was this guy, Bob Jones, who got up on stage. I didn't know who he was; to me he was just this little old man. And he started saying all these things and made this announcement that "an angel has just entered the building, and his name is Breakthrough."

He kept talking about where this angel came from and all this stuff. I'm just rolling my eyes at him, but everybody else in that place, and I mean two thousand-plus people, all are just going crazy—screaming and going crazy! I said to my wife, "These guys are insane."

The worship continued, so I closed my eyes—mostly because I didn't like watching the "charismania" that was happening all around me. Now up to this point I was not someone who "felt" things. I didn't "feel" the presence of God or "feel" the Holy Spirit—not like a lot of those people seemed to, that's for sure.

So I was standing there worshipping with my eyes closed, when somebody walked in front of me. I remember thinking, "That's weird," because at the time nobody was near me or around me.

I opened my eyes, but there was no one there. I closed my eyes again, and with my eyes shut I suddenly saw an angel. I had never seen an angel before, and I have never seen one since. I could see him only with my eyes closed. It was as if there was a darkness when I closed my eyes, and an even darker darkness, but I could see his out-line very, very clearly. I could see his forearm and that he was about two inches taller than I am. He was standing about five feet to my left, totally still. Then, suddenly, he turned and walked right up to me. And that's when I felt him, felt his presence, which was very unusual for me.

I remember leaning back, away from him, because of his presence—he was the most intense individual I have ever encoun-tered in my life.

Then he spoke to me; not audibly, but it was a voice I could hear in my head. It exploded, actually, in my head, and he asked me three times, "Are you ready?" And I answered three times, "Yes." I didn't know what I was saying yes to, I didn't know what I needed to be ready for.

After the third time I asked, "Ready for what?" because I was thinking, "What are you talking about?"

He just looked at me. I remember I couldn't see any features on his face, but it was like he was smoldering at me.

He said, "Make that movie."

And he walked away.

That angelic encounter was the impetus for my beginning the first of the three documentary movies I've made. I mean, if you have an angelic encounter, you realize it's time to stop messing around and get off your butt and actually do what the Lord has been asking you to do.

So three weeks later I was sitting down with Bill Johnson, senior pastor of Bethel Church in Redding, California, to do the very first interview for *Finger of God.*

Darren Wilson is an independent filmmaker, international speaker, and author. His first three films, Finger of God, Furious Love, *and* Father of Lights, *have been shown in thousands of churches and seen by millions of people worldwide. His next adventure film,* Holy Ghost, *is currently in production. Upcoming projects to be released through his production company, Wanderlust Productions (www.WPFilm.com), also include* The Greatest Fight *with UFC/WWE legend Ken Shamrock, and a cartoon titled* Anointed Fighters. *Darren and his wife, Jenell, live near Chicago, Illinois, with their three children, Serenity, Stryder, and River.*

ALL KINDS OF ANGELS

By Dennis Reanier

I PERSONALLY HAVE SEEN angels, all kinds of angels. I have seen some that are small, some that are large, and some that are gigantic. They are not all the same. I have seen angels who look just like a man and others who look more like a giant.

I have noticed that even though some angels appear to be small, they seem to carry the same amount of power as the larger angels. Their size doesn't necessarily seem to have anything to do with whether they have more or less power.

Angels are all around us all the time, but most people are unaware of it. Most people function with a lack of revelation, or what I would call a lack of spiritual eyes or spiritual senses.

The evidence that angels are all around us is in the Bible. Second Kings 6:16–18 is an account of when the prophet Elisha was with his personal servant in his tent. They were with the armies of Israel, which were fully surrounded by their enemies. The servant was looking all around, seeing only with his eyes, seeing only the things in the natural realm that were going on around them. He did not see the angelic realm. He was not seeing in the spiritual realm. He was completely unaware that the angels were there and that they were actually interacting with him and Elisha.

Elisha prayed for his servant's eyes to be opened to see the angelic realm, and he was stunned by what he saw—so many angels all working and fighting for them in a situation that, in the natural realm, seemed utterly hopeless. But with his eyes opened to see into the spiritual, angelic realm, he realized much more was actually happening, and it changed the way he thought and reacted in that situation.

In the same way we often do not have eyes to see into the spiritual or the supernatural realm. Instead, especially in the Western world, we have become more cognizant minded, more oriented to the material world, and we do not see in the spiritual realm. But the angels' realm is the spiritual one; they usually are not seen in the natural realm. The Bible calls them "ministering spirits" (Heb. 1:14), and that's exactly what they are—spirits, spirit beings.

I've seen angels in my room at night. They'll wake me up in the middle of the night, and I'll see them standing there, but they are so big that half their bodies are above the ceiling. They are huge, gigantic, enormous!

The angels who have appeared to me have often had wings, or what look like wings. But other angels look like they have no wings at all. Whether or not they have wings, or how many wings they have, can indicate what kind of angels they are. For example, cherubim and seraphim are multi-winged angels who minister more with the glory of God. So usually when they manifest or show up, they do so with a glory or a light about them.

And, honestly, it is a little bit startling when you first see angels.

When you wake up in the middle of the night, it takes some time for your spiritual eyes to see the angelic, and when you do, it's hard not to be startled. Over time I have become more peaceful with the encounters because I have grown to recognize that these guys are on my side! I have come to understand that they were appearing to me to minister to me, to be a messenger.

But they *are* supernatural, and seeing them can be intimidating when you're used to functioning only in the natural realm. But for me now functioning with them has become a more regular part of my life. It can become part of the way you operate, part of the way you live your life.

ANGELS IN HER HOME

By Joan Hunter

IN MY FAMILY angels have always been part of our lives. It's been really awesome. Recently we were in a service and saw them become part of another family's life.

A man was believing God for his marriage, for God to restore his marriage, and had asked us to pray particularly for the restoration. He had come to our service, but his wife had no interest and had stayed at home. Suddenly during the service his wife texted him.

He wondered what was going on because she knew he was at a church service, and he didn't know any reason why she would need to text him in the middle of it. So he got up to go outside to read the text.

She had sent him pictures of their home—with angelic beings that you could see in the texted pictures!

It turned out that right at the time we were praying for him, his wife, and their marriage, angels showed up in their home. Our prayer had been, "God, somehow we release the wife to You; show her that You are real." That is when these angels showed up in their house. The wife was able to see them with her own eyes, and because of that she believed that Jesus and God are real!

It was amazing.

It is a real sign, a real answer to prayer when angels show up in your home and you can take pictures of them and text the pictures!

THE ANGEL AT BIG SUR

By Doug Addison

I HAVE HAD ANGELIC encounters since I was a young kid. I didn't know what they were then, but now that I have been around the angels a lot more and worked with them, I understand that angels were visiting me when I was young.

I think a lot of children are visited by angels. Adults tend to tell them to "grow up," or they downplay what is really going on, and kids are not able to properly recognize the encounter.

My most distinct encounter was as an adult, however, at Big Sur, California, in 1991. God had spoken to me that I was going to have an encounter, but this one would be unlike any other I had ever experienced.

I was camping at Big Sur, and I took a walk in the woods, when suddenly I came across the presence of God. I walked right into it, and it just knocked me to the ground! It was so awesome.

But here's the important thing: at first I didn't realize this was an angelic encounter because I didn't see anything. I didn't see an angel, but this presence knocked me on the ground—I was lying flat on the path in the woods and couldn't even lift my head. Then the angel spoke into my spirit, not aloud or audibly, but into my spirit; I could hear it just as clearly as if it were speaking aloud.

It gave me a very powerful message about things that were coming to the earth and about a change that was going to happen. I had a whole encounter, hearing and receiving a big message. I wrote it all down, but then the Lord said to me, "Seal it up and do not tell any-body until you see these things come about."

And over the years I would think about how all my friends were getting to write angel books, but my message had to stay sealed. It wasn't until 2004 that those things came to pass, so I just kept a file folder full of information, full of revelation.

Then in 2004, as all these things the angel had told me about began coming to pass, I was permitted to release the prophetic word. And it was all through my very first, distinct angelic encounter.

But you know, for the longest time it bothered me that I hadn't seen the angel. I wondered about that, so I started researching other biblical encounters to compare them with mine. Also, I had started having other encounters, and I wanted to understand them and be sure what they were. Sometimes I would see angels and other times I would not. So I studied the word *angel* in the New Testament to learn the way different angelic encounters were experienced and described.

I found that in Acts 10 Cornelius says he had an encounter at three o'clock in the afternoon, and he distinctly saw the angel. But in Acts 12 when an angel was physically helping Peter to be released from prison, Peter was unsure in that moment if he had seen an angel and thought he might have just been having a vision. That's when it dawned on me: "Wow! Here we have times when we might distinctly see something and other times when it might seem to us more like a dream or a vision." So we can have either experience.

I also found that sometimes we encounter angels, but at other times our encounter is with the Holy Spirit. So our encounters can be different all the time.

DÉJÀ VU

By Doug Addison

I HAVE SO MANY angel stories! One really profound encounter occurred in 2004 when I was living in Los Angeles—the "City of Angels."

It was the middle of the night, and I was asleep in bed. I remember waking up and feeling something brush against my ear. I was lying on my right side, and I know I was awake because I looked over, saw the clock, and saw my wife lying there asleep. Then I saw this brilliant white light in the room.

And the presence of God was so thick in the room. Then I kind of peeked up to see over me, and hovering right there over me was everything you would expect when seeing an angel. This angel was translucent, glowing white but with long golden braids. I saw the features only for a nanosecond, but the sight is etched in my spirit. The angel was holding back long golden braids and was speaking into my ear with beautiful golden lips.

He was hovering, just as you would expect an angel to hover, and wearing a golden sash that was also very white. And in that moment, I did what any man of God would do—I screamed!

It startled me. You know, those encounters don't come with a disclaimer like, "An angelic encounter from Me, the Lord, is coming in...three—two—one." They don't come like that. They are startling!

In fact, when the Bible describes an encounter, more often than not people either fell down like they're dead or the angels tell them, "Fear not," because these things will rock your world!

So yeah, I yelled and woke up my wife, and the angel just vanished. My wife said when she woke up she did see the angel. She could see a presence in the corner of the room. But I felt disappointed because I could not remember what the angel whispered in my ear.

There will never be a TV show in which the announcer says, "Doug's going to tell us what the angel said right after this break," because I do not remember. But I have come to understand something about angelic encounters. Now years later I understand that when we have encounters or when we hear from the Lord, whether it is God speaking to us through the Holy Spirit or by an angel, it does not matter if we remember it. God is Spirit. He deposits things into our spirits. Now as I look back, I realize the timing of that encounter. Right after it I began getting revelation.

When the angel whispered in my ear, he was whispering revelation into my spirit. It does not matter that I can't remember it with my mind.

In fact, the revelation the angel gave me that night became a book I wrote about how to help people find their destiny. I associate that revelation download with that angelic encounter.

I believe this is what it means in the account from Job 33:14–17, when the Bible says: "For God may speak in one way, or in another, yet man does not perceive it. In a dream, in a vision of the night, when deep sleep falls upon men, while slumbering on their beds, then He opens the ears of men, and seals their instruction. In order to turn man from his deed, and conceal pride from man."

Sometimes God will speak clearly; other times it will be sealed away.

When you have an angelic encounter and it is sealed away inside you so that you don't remember it, it is very similar to having a dream that you can't remember. Then later on you realize you're in the middle of living these things out, and suddenly you feel like you're having déjà vu.

I am convinced that déjà vu is our experiencing or remembering what God has spoken to us ahead of time. There has been either an angelic encounter or something has happened and it has been sealed up until the moment you begin experiencing what was sealed.

THE HEAVENLY SCEPTER

By Doug Addison

Recently I was at a church service on a Sunday morning. I wasn't the speaker on that particular morning, so I was worshipping, and the presence of the Lord came. In fact, I felt the presence come suddenly, and when it did, I held my hands out in front of me and felt an angel touching them.

I closed my eyes and could see the angel standing in front of me. I did not want to open my eyes because I did not want the angel, or my ability to see it, go away. The angel then grabbed my hands, and I could see into heaven, in real time. It was like watching a video of what was happening in heaven.

I was watching a ceremony in which my mom, who had passed away in 1999, was receiving her crown of glory. The moment the angel touched my hands, I could see this happening. It was the most awesome thing.

My mom looked like Esther from the Old Testament. That's the only way I can describe it. She wore a long robe with a very long white train and a crown on her head, angels standing around her, and they put a scepter into her hand.

Now, two things I should mention about my mom: she was a jokester, and she couldn't drive a stick-shift car. When the angels put the scepter in her hand, she began moving it all around, and it reminded me of her being unable to drive a stick shift.

As she moved the scepter all around, things would light up wherever she pointed it. Things in heaven would light up, and angels would respond with sounds or with singing. The angels standing with her, who had given her the scepter, steadied her hand, showing her how to lean the scepter toward something.

In the distance I could see the throne room. As she moved the scepter and learned to lean it toward the throne, the throne would light up in the distance. As it did, resources from heaven would be sent off according to the request.

After the angels worked with her for a few minutes, suddenly my mom yelled, "Give it to Doug!" Instantly, because my hands were stretched out toward the angel, I suddenly had the scepter in my hand. This was taking place in the spiritual realm, but I could feel the scepter in my hand.

The moment the scepter was in my hands, I "came to" and realized I was back in the meeting. I fell over onto my wife because the power of God was so strong.

To this day when I hold out my hands I feel the burning of the scepter. And to this day I have a new authority with prayer. I am very cautious of whom I speak this authority over.

I have inherited several things from my mother when she died. One is her evangelistic gift, another is her prophetic gift, and one other is her Bible. The Bible is the one she kept with her through her illness and invalidity and hospice care. It is very tattered.

Well after that encounter on Sunday morning, I went home and found my mom's Bible opened to Esther 5. I had not opened it to that place, but when I came home it was opened. Esther 5 is about the time Esther went before the king and "when the king saw Queen Esther standing in the court...she found favor in his sight, and the king held out to Esther the golden scepter that was in his hand" (v. 2).

That was an awesome encounter!

I COULD SMELL THE SULFUR

By Steven Springer

M Y FIRST EXPERIENCE with the angelic happened almost immediately after I was saved. Suddenly the unseen realm was opened to me, and I began to see not only the angelic but also the demonic.

I remember one time in particular when God was opening my heart to see into the unseen. That particular night my wife, Renee, and I were praying together in bed. It was just a closing prayer of our day. I looked up at the ceiling fan at one point, and suddenly the fan began to get farther and farther and farther away from me. I was taken into an atmosphere, into a kind of chamber. The closest comparison I can make is to the catacombs in Rome—like a large corridor.

My spirit was being lifted, being removed from my body, and I was seeing and standing in the unseen, spiritual realm, but my wife who was next to me in our bed could hear everything I was saying as I described what was going on.

I was standing in this corridor, when a massive angel came and took me by the hand and led me down the corridor. As we moved along, there was a shaft of light that reached from the floor all the way to the ceiling. It was beaming, and the farther we got down the corridor, the more the texture of the walls changed. It changed from rough, carved-out rock to polished marble. At one point the walls became translucent.

As we moved closer to the light, I began to feel a presence, the presence of the Lord. He was leading me on, farther and farther, right toward the light. When I got to the light, He pointed up. As I looked up, I could hardly see because the light was so intense and so bright. It was painful to my eyes to look into this light. Then out of nowhere a dove landed on my shoulder and said to me, "Turn around."

I turned around; one moment I was in the corridor, and the next moment there was a large chasm right in front of me. In fact, I nearly fell. I was trying to catch myself from actually falling into a pit. In that moment I suddenly felt heat and smelled sulfur.

I was standing on the edge of a rock, and I could smell the sulfur and feel the heat, when suddenly I heard a *woomp*. I saw something flash past me, then another *woomp*, and another flash of something going past me. At first I couldn't figure out what was going on. But when my eyes were really opened, I could see plainly that people were flying by me, falling into the pit. The dove on my shoulder said, "Pay attention. Pay attention."

I could see the images and faces of the people as they fell past me. Their faces are still etched in my mind today. I was trying to figure out if this was real. I was asking, "God, is this real? What I am seeing right now?"

At one point these people were reaching out to me and hitting my arms as they went by, crying out, "Help me! Help me! Help me! Help me!" Their cries were desperate as they literally were being released into the abyss. I asked, "God, how can this be?" He answered, "They chose to live a life without Me. I did not send them there; it was the choice they chose."

In His voice, in His answer, I could feel the heart of the Father. I could feel His compassion, and I began to weep.

The next thing I knew, I was back next to my wife in my bed. I was weeping, and I wept and wept.

The entire reason for the encounter—for the angel to show me those things and for the Holy Spirit, represented by the dove, to lead me to that place—was to open my eyes. It was so I would see the truth of the importance of our going out and sharing the good news.

Seeing it, seeing the reality of what is going on, broke my heart. To see it that way, to see the reality of it, broke my heart to understand how important it is for us to evangelize and tell people about the good news of Jesus. The angels and the Holy Spirit are urging us; they have a message for us to take to the world.

That encounter opened up my whole world so that I now run hard after one thing: sharing the good news of Jesus with people.

Steven Springer and his wife, Rene, are the senior leaders of Global Presence Ministries (www.GlobalPresence.com), an apostolic ministry based in Madison, Wisconsin. Part of the Apostolic Council of Prophetic Elders, Steven and Rene have seen thousands of people saved, delivered, and healed as they have ministered throughout the United States and internationally in countries such as Ghana, Uganda, India, Israel, Italy, and Russia.

WHAT WAS THAT?

By Robert Hotchkin

EVERY DECEMBER I take time away for prayer—my own prayer
retreat. One year some friends let me use their beach cottage in
North Carolina. Of course in December nobody's on the beach, so I
would go on walks and talk with God.

Before that particular December prayer retreat my whole ministry focus had been on leading missions trips and outreaches in
Pattaya, Thailand. We were invading that city because it is known
for its sex trade. People from all over the world joined us as we went
into brothels and bars and saw God do amazing things. We saw salvations, miracles, and healings. God was glorified.

Well, back at the cottage one night I was in prayer. From where
I was sitting I could see across the room into the kitchen. I was
praying for Southeast Asia, for Thailand, and Cambodia, when suddenly I looked up and across the room and saw a massive flash of
light! I saw it with open eyes, with my natural eyes—a massive flash
of light in the room, totally real.

What's funny is, even though I was on a prayer retreat, even
though I was focused on the Lord and deep in prayer, my first
thought was not "That was an angel" or "I'm having a supernatural
encounter." It was "What was that?"

I stood up and walked into the kitchen, thinking the ballast of
the fluorescent lights had blown out. I thought I was going to have
to change a bulb or something. And I am so not handy. I don't even
know what a ballast is; I just know it's the name of something in
fluorescent lights that can blow out.

As I was walking across the room, God suddenly dropped a prophetic word in my mind about Europe. I instantly started praying
for Europe—prophesying over Europe and all its nations.

The word just kept coming and coming and coming until, when it
finished, I said again, "What was that?" I had never thought about

Europe. I did not feel a calling to Europe. I didn't have a passion for Europe. But suddenly I now had a burning inside me for Europe to come to know the Lord. I had a burning desire to speak to the nations of Europe and to its people. Then the next thing I knew, God took me in a vision to Europe and showed me many things.

What is amazing to me is it all began with that flash of light.

I am a big believer that everything that comes to us supernaturally must be rooted and grounded in the Word of God. In fact, the more supernatural something is, the more we need to be rooted and grounded in the Word because the Word is our plumb line.

So to have confidence in what I had experienced, I started reading the Bible and praying, "God, You have to show this to me in the Word. I do not know what that was. What was that flash of light?"

Well, Hebrews 1 declares that God "makes His angels spirits and His ministers a flame of fire" (Heb. 1:7). The word *flame* in Greek means "flame" or "flash." So we know from this verse that God's angels can appear as flashes of fire and light. That confirmed for me the flash was an angel.

Then I asked about the sudden experience of prophesying over the nations. God showed me Revelation 10, in which He ordained an encounter between the apostle John and an angel. God told John that the angel had a scroll for him—or, in other words, a message. John went to the angel to receive it, and when he did, the angel basically told him, "Now I want you to eat this. It is going to be sweet on your lips, but then it will be sour in your stomach." (See Revelation 10:1–9.)

John obeyed. He took the scroll, the message, and put it in his mouth and swallowed it. In other words, he took the message from the Lord, through the angel, and digested it, and it became a part of him. Then God told John, "Now you must prophesy to the nations and to the peoples." (See Revelation 10:10–11.)

Isn't that amazing? That passage confirmed to me, through the plumb line of the Word, that God uses His angels, those flashes of light, to bring us a message that we can receive so that it becomes a part of who we are. Then we speak those things forth on God's behalf to impact people and nations around the world.

It happened to me, right there in that cottage living room on the beach in North Carolina. God gave me a message through His angel, the flash of light, and it was a message for Europe, which He then had me speak out. It is amazing to me how things in the atmosphere, in the spiritual realm, over nations began to shift from an encounter I had.

Here's where it got really interesting for me. God called me to Europe. In the last couple of years my ministry focus has shifted, and I am now a traveling itinerant minister in Europe. At one point I spent eight out of eleven months living in Europe.

It is just amazing to me how God can do that, how out of the flash of light that I thought was a blown bulb, God sent an angelic messenger to download a message for the nations of Europe, and then He shifted my ministry focus.

God sent that bright light. We see it in the Bible account about the apostle Peter. When he was imprisoned, the Lord set him free by sending an angel, who showed up as a bright light appeared in the cell. (See Acts 12:7.) So for some reason God's angels are often associated with light.

That was my experience: a bright flash of light, and then suddenly I received a scroll, a message from God, that became part of me, and I started speaking forth things to the nations, which affected shifts in the earth and a shift to my calling from Southeast Asia to Europe.

It is great how God uses His angels. One of their roles seems to be helping us to come into the calling God has on each of our lives—helping us become the full expression of God and His gospel, which is what we were created to be in Christ.

Think about Mary and the angel Gabriel. Gabriel went to Mary and basically said to her, "This is what is going to happen for you: the Lord is going to visit you and the Spirit of God will come upon you, and you are going to actually become impregnated with Emmanuel; you will bring forth the Messiah."

Here we see Gabriel's role, his ministry to Mary. It was to prepare her for the great call on her life. At the end of Gabriel's explanation of what was going to happen, Mary said, "Let it be to me according to your word" (Luke 1:38). Mary's encounter is a model for us: we see angels who are sent to help prepare us, to aid us for what God has called us to. It happened to Mary. It happened to me in that cottage in North Carolina. It can happen to you.

Robert Hotchkin ministers with Patricia King's XP Ministries (www .XPMinistries.com). His preaching, teaching, and ministry inspire believers to take hold of their restored relationship with the Father through the finished work of the cross and walk the earth as Jesus did, destroying every work of darkness everywhere they go.

I THOUGHT IT WAS JUST
MY IMAGINATION

By Gretchen Rodriguez

SEEING ANGELS WASN'T normal for me until I made a decision that because people throughout the Bible could see and talk with angels, I should be able to as well. I began asking the Lord to open my spiritual eyes and allow me to see what He would like me to see. Then I began looking around the room when I would go to meetings or be in times of personal prayer. I was expecting to see angels in the same way I could see people—with my physical eyes.

When I began encountering angels, I was excited; however, I couldn't see them the way I had anticipated. Instead of seeing them with my eyes, I had only a "knowing" that angels were present. As you can imagine, this left me with a lot of doubts about whether or not I was actually seeing them—or if it was just my imagination.

Many times I would know the moment angels would enter the room. I could sense if they were tall, short, had wings or not, and also know why they had come. Many times in meetings I would see them ministering to people or handing them gifts, but I was too afraid to tell anyone because I wasn't sure if what I sensed was just my imagination. The Lord, however, was faithful to help me understand what was happening.

One evening I was watching an online teaching by prophetic minister Patricia King. Suddenly I sensed a huge warrior angel drop into my room and stand about three feet away from me holding a sword across his chest. I knew what he was wearing, knew that he was about seven to eight feet tall, and I knew why he was there.

At first I was excited, but because I couldn't actually see him, I decided it was probably all in my mind. As soon as I made that decision, Patricia said, "Someone just felt a warrior angel come into the room! It's standing right by you, and you think it's your imagination, but the Lord wants you to know it isn't your imagination."

I was stunned! The video I was watching wasn't live; it was recorded. The Lord knew ahead of time that I would be watching this particular video and spoke to Patricia at the time she was recording it to encourage me. It certainly did encourage me! Not only did the Lord speak to me that I indeed saw an angel, but He also made me feel loved and special, knowing that He took the time to plan the whole thing way in advance so I would trust what I was beginning to walk in.

It is hard to explain how, though I was not seeing angels with my natural eyes, I knew the details I knew. It felt very much like I was making it all up in my mind. Since I couldn't literally see the angels, I wondered how I possibly could trust that what I was sensing was real.

The next thing that happened was a series of events that truly confirmed in my heart that I do indeed see angels.

About six months after seeing the warrior angel, my husband and I went to a weeklong conference with multiple speakers and many thousands of attendees. Each service I would go up front during the worship times, and each service I would know where the angels were and what they were doing. However, by the time I attended the conference, I again was doubting that what I was seeing was real. I had begun to think it was a product of my creative imagination.

During the conference I sensed many different things, not only angels but also colors swirling around people, clouds covering the stage, and winds blowing across people's faces and bodies. Each time that I would sense something and begin to doubt it, one of the conference leaders would interrupt worship to announce what he or she was seeing in the spirit. Without fail, every day, every meeting I attended, whatever I was seeing, they would announce they were seeing the very same thing!

By the fifth day of the conference all I could do was laugh! The Lord was sending me a message loud and clear, and I repented for my unbelief and vowed never again to doubt what I was seeing.

The last day we were at the conference, the event was being held outside in a baseball stadium, and we were sitting in the stands. On the left side of the field where the stage was were quite a number of children who were dancing and jumping all around, worshipping the Lord. Suddenly I could see that angels were dancing and playing with the children! This time I didn't doubt but thoroughly enjoyed the scene.

Then something caught my attention on the opposite side of the field where the main entrance was. Onto the field walked Jesus! Even from high up in the stands I could see the smile on His face—it was radiant. He walked behind the large stage, toward where the children and angels were dancing, and though I could sense His delight in seeing them, He seemed very focused.

He then turned toward the stage, went up the stairs, and stood next to the main speaker. At that moment the people in the stands began to erupt with such loud, spontaneous shouts of praise, I don't believe I will ever forget it. Over approximately eight thousand people spontaneously shouting praises even louder than the music literally caused me to feel the reverberation of their praise in my body.

The blessing of being able to see what was happening in the spirit, the very reason for the eruption—Jesus—blessed me more than words can convey. Just when I thought it couldn't get any better, the speaker ran to the microphone. With excitement he explained that he saw Jesus enter the field through the entrance, walk behind the stage, and come up the stairs to where he was standing. Exactly what I had seen!

The crowd burst into praise. All I could do was sit there with tears of joy streaming down my face, never again to doubt my beautiful gift of seeing in the spirit.

Most of us have had moments when we chalked up to our imagination something that actually might have been spiritual. My prayer is to encourage you to begin trusting what you have seen. If you have never sensed things like this and would like to, I would like to pray over you the 2 Kings 6:17 prayer that Elisha prayed over his servant: "Lord, I pray, open his eyes that he may see."

Gretchen Rodriguez (www.BurningHearts333.blogspot.com) is a prophetic ballet dancer who teaches prophetic dance at workshops in the United States and internationally. She and her family were missionaries to Puerto Rico for nine years. Now she and her husband, Len, live in Redding, California, with their three daughters, Bianca, Karina, and Isabela.

ANGELIC AND HOLY SPIRIT ENCOUNTERS

By Doug Addison

IN 2009 WHILE I was in Cape Town, South Africa, I had a series of angelic encounters for an entire week that blew me away. At that point I had to start studying the angelic encounters because I was used to hearing from the Holy Spirit, through my prophetic gifting, but in South Africa I was having encounters in which I was hearing from angels, and I knew it was different. So I took notes.

I made notes every time I would hear a revelation and every time I would receive a prophetic message through the Holy Spirit. I noticed that sometimes it was almost like it came from outside, while other times it came from within me.

I was able to determine that the times when I heard from within, from inside me, were more likely to be from the Holy Spirit. But the other times when I heard more from the outside—when it's almost audible but not quite because the messenger is still speaking to your spirit—then those encounters were more likely to be angelic messengers.

Today most people have just become used to listening and encountering the Holy Spirit, but we forget that there are also ministering angels. The angels are not omnipresent like the Holy Spirit. That's why they will feel like they come from outside rather than inside.

When I studied this for biblical perspective, I found that in Acts 8:26–39, when Philip had an evangelistic encounter with an Ethiopian eunuch, that verse 26 tells us an angel told Philip to go down to the road, and when he got there the Spirit spoke to him and told him to walk over to the chariot (v. 29).

So this is an example of the interaction and collaboration between the angels and the Holy Spirit working together.

YOUR OWN SUPERNATURAL ENCOUNTERS

By Doug Addison

T HERE ARE MANY different kinds of encounters we can have in the spirit—encounters with angels, with the Lord, and with the Holy Spirit. Understanding or discerning which ones they are is for us to discover.

When the apostle Paul said we are the body of Christ, he was saying there are different roles for each of us, different aspects to each part, but one body (1 Cor. 12:12). God is the same way. He is one God but with different aspects. He is Father. He is Son. He is Holy Spirit.

People are always saying, "It's all about Jesus," and yes, it is. Don't get me wrong. But there are other aspects to God that we may encounter.

We also have ministering angels who do things at a level that we could never do. We need them to line things up and to be on the defensive for us. We see this, for example, in the Book of Daniel where the angel came, but only after he had been resisted by the demonic angel and prevented from bringing his message (Dan. 10:13).

So we do know that there is spiritual warfare going on. Of course, the Holy Spirit trumps it all, but there is an aspect to God that people do not understand, and it is this: God is just. He is a just God. If He forced Himself on anybody, then He would be a dictator. So that is why He has to allow everything to play out. Angels, demons, the Holy Spirit—they all have a role to play out. It is because God is just that He must allow it to happen. Too many people do not realize that.

I've seen both sides, by the way. I came out of the occult in the 1980s, out of deep darkness. But the things that I see in the spiritual realms now, now that I am in the kingdom of light, are way beyond anything I ever saw previously. The amount of power, visions, revelation—now it is all clothed in love. God is love.

Most people try to discern whether an encounter or presence is God or the enemy, the devil. I say it's easy. God is love. So for me, I spend my time trying to discern whether I am encountering an angel or the Holy Spirit, God the Father, or just something coming from myself. Those are the things I have been working on discerning.

The only way that I have found to be effective in learning to discern how to hear and what source I am hearing from—whether from angelic messengers or the Holy Spirit of the Father or the Son—is by journaling. I take notes and journal every day of my life.

Take today, for instance. I journaled today for yesterday. I filled in yesterday's journal, but I went back and journaled all the things I learned—from a future standpoint.

I recommend journaling by making notes on how the encounter felt. By that I mean, go back to the last time you really heard God, that you know you heard God. Then sit down and write about it. How did it come to you? How did it feel? Was it from the outside in, or was it from the inside out? Was there a certain kind of presence?

You will then have different encounters to compare, and you will learn from them. This is how you will learn to discern your own supernatural encounters.

THE BRUSH OF ANGEL WINGS

By Melissa Fisher

MANY PEOPLE ARE afraid of the spiritual realm; they are afraid of the supernatural. They are afraid because they can't control it, or they can't reason with it, or it doesn't make any sense to them. But I would submit to them that, as the Word tells us, the gospel of Christ is "foolishness to those who are perishing" (1 Cor. 1:18). You *can't* explain it.

Who can *really* explain salvation? You pray to this guy who died for you two thousand years ago, and then you're supposed be able to go to heaven? On its face, that doesn't make any sense!

But the Word also says the ways of the Lord are past finding out (Rom. 11:33). So if you can reason what God is, then you have Him in a box, and you need to expand it. Why do I say these things? Because the supernatural realm, the spiritual realm, is past our being able to reason it, get a handle on it, or even explain it.

It is bigger than we are. God is bigger than we are. Yes, the unknown does freak people out, and sometimes it *is* scary, but when we start to embrace the unknown, it makes the life that we have been given so much more exciting! It gives you the opportunity to not be afraid, but to explore.

I always recommend that people ask of the Lord, "Lord, take me into these experiences," because He says He will not give you a scorpion if you ask for something good (Luke 11:12). What that means is, if you ask Him to give you an experience in the heavenly realm, in His kingdom, He is not going to lead you into something evil. He is not going to give you a bad gift.

Open spiritual senses—seeing into the heavenly realm, seeing into the assignments of angels—are gifts, gifts God has given to us, and He would never give you a bad gift. That's why I encourage people: don't be afraid. Don't be afraid. Go with God.

Let Him take you by the hand, and let Him take you on this

experience with Himself. If you ask Him that, and if you ask in faith, knowing that He is a good God and He would not give you anything bad, then you will go on the ride of your life with Him, and He will begin to show you all these things. And you will be so amazed! I tell you for sure, you will be opened up and fulfilled at the same time.

When I started to seek the Lord about opening my spiritual senses, I began by praying, "God, You are no respecter of persons, and if You have given that gift of feeling or seeing to somebody else, then I believe it is for me too. I open myself up to whatever it is that You would like to do, Lord. I call on You and ask to be able to see what everybody else is seeing."

When I am in a meeting and see people shaking, crying, or having whatever experience they are having, I choose to believe. I press in to what God is doing in them and in their hearts to see if He will do that for me.

And, really, that was where it all began.

I would see something going on in one part of the room, and I would say, "Lord, what's going on over there? Will You let me see it? Will You let me feel that?" And He did; He started to. It was very small in the beginning, but as it happened I would pray, "Thank You, Lord! Thank You for letting me have that."

As I did that, it was like I was celebrating Him, and as you celebrate and honor what He is doing, He'll do even more.

Now the Lord lets me see the angelic realm with my eyes open. I see visions, and I feel a lot in the Spirit as well. In fact, I was at a conference once and the glory got so amazingly deep that I could feel the presence of angels everywhere—so much so that when I walked down the hall I could feel their wings brushing me. Wherever I was, I could feel them crammed together, and it brought such joy and excitement that I could barely contain myself. That was an amazing angelic encounter.

Melissa Fisher serves as an administrator, intercessor, and itinerant speaker for Beth Teshuvah (www.bethteshuvah.com), a healing and intercessory ministry. Her passion is to see the body of Christ walk in the destiny God designed for the church from before the foundation of the world. She believes that through intimacy with God, repentance, intercession, and praise, all believers can become mature and live the abundant life Jesus came to give them.

A SUPERNATURAL LIFESTYLE

By Pam Crowder-Archibald

For the last twelve months I have been in a season of very intense angelic experiences, and they are happening often. It is unprecedented in my personal experience.

For me the Holy Spirit usually precedes the angelic visitation. I can tell which one is present by spiritual discernment; the Holy Spirit and angels feel or present themselves differently. At other times I can see who is there with my eyes. When the Holy Spirit comes, it is with a word or a message before the angels show up.

My encounters are full-on, open-eye, seeing with my natural eyes as angelic beings enter this physical realm and reveal themselves. In these visitations the angels have never spoken to me directly. Either I hear the voice of the Lord, or the Holy Spirit speaks to my spirit. When the angels come, they usually are watching me, or they are interacting in such a way that a message is being deposited into my spirit without words being spoken.

One of the reasons I believe God has increased the intensity and regularity of angelic visitations is not for my benefit only but because He wants to let all of us know that the supernatural realm should be a part of our everyday life. The angelic, the spiritual realm, is not something that you just go to church and experience; but even in your profession, in your work place, in your everyday you must be able to discern the spiritual realm.

There is a whole world behind the visible realm. It is the invisible realm, and God wants everybody to be aware of it and to walk in it. There is no reason a person should not be able to discern and interact in the invisible realm.

And this is not happening to me because I am someone special. I am not a special person. I don't have a huge ministry, and I am not famous. I am a lawyer, but I have just an average law practice. I don't have any superstar celebrity clients or this or that.

But that is the beauty of it! God puts His extraordinary in our ordinary. It is not about who you are, or how many television appearances you have done, or how many books you have written. It is simply this, that you have a love for Jesus and He wants to share the kingdom of God with you! That's it! God is going to open it up to you.

There is also no need to be afraid of the supernatural realm or the supernatural power of God. Having said that, whenever I have had an experience with angels, and I mean every single experience, it did bring the fear of the Lord. But let me clarify, the "fear of the Lord" is different from a "fear of the encounter." I want to be sure to make that point. I am not afraid of the encounter. I love the encounter. But there is a phenomenon that occurs when the natural realm is invaded by the presence of God's holy angels—it brings such total awe of the magnificence of our Lord and Savior.

You cannot explain or teach how an encounter feels or how it affects you. You cannot preach it in church or teach it in a Bible study. You must have an encounter, which God has made available to us all. You must experience the encounter to understand it. And God does want to share it with us because we are not really from the earthly realm anyway. We are from heaven, and He desires us to experience heaven.

God wants us to partake of these things of heaven while we are on earth. The notion that we are to incorporate the angelic into a lifestyle of encountering God and His holy angels is part of the kingdom of God on earth the way that it exists in heaven.

This is the thing about encounters: it's not about the encounter; it has a divine purpose beyond just that moment, that feeling, that experience. There is a purpose in it for us to walk in, to carry, to understand, with something for us to do in the season of time we are in.

The supernatural truth is that God really does heal, He really does deliver, and the angels really do show up. In fact, they love to show up. But the thing about it is that we as believers have to be open to it. We have to desire it, we have to want that, and we have to understand the transition and the integration of the Word of God in us.

The angels, the spiritual realm, the unseen realm, are not just a bunch of empty words. They are reality. We have an opportunity to integrate them into our lifestyle. If you go to church or read the Bible but have a dull, boring Christian life, then the Word of God has not been integrated into your lifestyle. The Word says God will "give His angels charge over you" (Ps. 91:11). If that were integrated into our lifestyle, we would be familiar with His angels and interact with them.

I firmly believe there are groups of angels who are waiting to be reassigned and reactivated to the saints. It is as if, for some reason, the saints of light, that's us as Christians, have not been utilizing the angelic forces as much as we should.

And when it comes to the area of spiritual warfare, I believe that in the next season of revival for the harvest, in the end times, we must utilize the full force of the heavenly angelic forces. We have to in order to do what we cannot as humans do in our own physical bodies, in our physical realm. This is partnering with the angelic to assist us in doing what we cannot do.

Pam Crowder-Archibald (www.TakeLegalAuthorityBlog.com) is an attorney, author, legal analyst, and apostolic minister. She has practiced law in several states for the last eighteen years and is a former assistant attorney general. She ministers throughout the United States and internationally, emphasizing healing and deliverance, spiritual warfare, city transformation, apostolic and prophetic ministry, and the anointing of God's laws. She lives in Phoenix, Arizona, with her daughter.

PART 3

MINISTERING SPIRITS

Are they not all ministering spirits sent forth to
minister for those who will inherit salvation?
—Hebrews 1:14

THE ANGEL IN THE NURSERY

By Elizabeth A. Nixon, Esq.

M Y FAVORITE ANGELIC encounter was when my son was three months old—and, really, it was his encounter.

I was in that stage as a new mother when I tried to let him fall asleep by himself. One night I had fed him, rocked him, put him down, and closed the nursery door, but I had the baby monitor on so I could hear him at the other end of the house.

I heard him stirring and crying, and I thought, "I'll just let this go." As he continued to cry, I heard footsteps walking across the room and a hand patting him on the back and a voice softly saying, "*Shhh.*" Instantly I thought, "Oh, my husband's gone up there to check on him." So I went down the hall, but my husband was at the other end of the house, and the baby's nursery door was still closed. No one had gone into my son's room.

I knew in that moment I had heard an angel walking across the room and comforting my son!

What's great for me is that I know in the future my son will need the Lord's protection—he'll need for the angelic to be with him—and from the encounter in his nursery I have a precedent for knowing he'll be protected in the future. I also have an account to share with him to teach him that the Lord and His angels are really there, always, and they will interact with him.

Elizabeth A. Nixon, Esq., is an attorney, author, and speaker with a heart to help others discover their divine destiny. The founder of Nixon Law Corp., a Los Angeles boutique law firm, Nixon has been featured in Vanity Fair *magazine and has received the National Business Woman of the Year Award. Through her ministry, White Quill Media (www.WhiteQuillMedia.com), she also ministers across the country. She is the author of* Inspired by the Psalms.

THE COLOR OF ANGELS

By Elizabeth A. Nixon, Esq.

Gᴏᴅ'ꜱ ᴘᴜʀᴘᴏꜱᴇ ɪɴ releasing angels into the earth to interact with us is for the singular goal of establishing the kingdom of heaven on earth. In that process angels' interaction with us serves several functions, but all functions are toward that one goal.

We know from the Book of John that angels ascend into the heavens to get what we need and then descend from the heavens to bring it to us. Angels are often called ministering spirits in the Bible, assigned by God to us (Heb. 1:14). Their goal is to help us get into alignment with the kingdom of heaven.

We know from the Book of Psalms that they are to obey the Word of God and the voice of the Word of God. The voice of the Word is our speaking God's purposes and promises. When we speak those things, we release angels to perform God's purposes in our lives.

Those are some of their functions, all working toward the goal that Jesus taught us in the Lord's Prayer: "Your kingdom come. Your will be done on earth as it is in heaven" (Matt. 6:10). When we are in alignment with the kingdom of heaven, we are released into our highest spiritual destiny.

These are the things I know from the Word. But I am also learning a lot about angels from my three-year-old son!

He interacts with the angelic realm all the time. Because I don't see them with my natural eyes the same way he does, I'm always asking him questions, especially at night when we're going to bed.

One night I asked him about my angel. "What color is Mummy's angel?" I asked. I expected it to be white because usually he talks about angels being white.

But this night he said, "Mummy, your angel is green." I thought, "Well, that's interesting because biblically green is associated with growth and prosperity." I liked that my angel was green. It showed me I was in a season of growth and of things becoming fruitful.

Another night, though, he said my angel was orange. In the Word orange often is associated with courage and perseverance. This gave me some clarity, especially in light of circumstances I was in the middle of with work and business.

We know that angels ascend and descend with the gifts we need in a season. Understanding that my angel was orange, knowing its color, gave me an idea of what God was bringing me in that season. I knew that His purpose was to bring me into alignment with His kingdom and my destiny—with what He was calling me into. That night, when I had an orange angel, I knew extra courage was on the way!

HOT SPOTS

By Doug Addison

In 2009 I was invited to speak at a conference in South Africa, and I knew God was going to speak to me very clearly while I was there. One of the things He showed me during the conference was how angels work and how it differs from the way the presence of God manifests.

One of my gifts is the gift of observation, meaning I can watch something or someone and see what God is doing. During the meetings I used this gift and watched the audience. I saw that there were different areas of the room, different areas in the congregation, where the presence of God was really strong. I noticed that people were touched in certain areas of the room more than in other areas.

So I would walk over to one of those "hot spots" and stand there. When I did, I could feel the presence of God very strongly. I began to experiment with it. I would pull people over to that area, and sure enough, they would be touched deeply, or they would be healed, just by being in that particular spot.

The Holy Spirit showed me this was happening because an angel was standing in that spot. You see, God—the Holy Spirit— is omnipresent, meaning He is everywhere at once. But angels are not omnipresent. They can be in only one place at a time. So when they were in a specific place in the room, that's where the healing and ministry would be especially strong.

HE TOOK OFF RUNNING!

By Faytene Grasseschi

M Y FIRST VIVID encounter with an angel happened when I was with a group of young people ministering on the inner-city streets of Vancouver, British Columbia.

We had a "prayer booth," and the young people were praying for street people who stopped at our booth. What was so sweet for me about this encounter was that these young adults had never done anything like this before. They were stepping out into something totally new to them. They were not "professional" prayer people!

I'll never forget what happened as we prayed for one street guy. Suddenly, as we were praying, his eyes just expanded like dinner plates, and he just stared at an area right behind our prayer team. He was fixated, like he was seeing something.

We realized that he was looking at something, and it was freaking him out! We didn't know exactly what was happening because he just ran off before we could ask him—he *booked* it out of there.

Later he came back and told us he had gone back to his room and had an encounter with the Lord. He said that while the young people were praying for him, loving on him, and giving him encouraging words, he had an open vision of what was standing right behind them. He had seen, with his eyes, the angel who was there to release God's presence.

Hebrews 1:14 says, "Are they not all ministering spirits sent forth to minister for those who will inherit salvation?" So I think his encounter was a manifestation of that. God dispatched an angel to help us minister to this guy, who ended up getting saved through seeing the angel.

The vision was more of a secondhand encounter for me because I only saw the guy react to the angel; I didn't see the angel myself. But I saw how it really impacted this guy and led him to Jesus. It was amazing!

Faytene Grasseschi serves as the pioneering director of TheCRY Movement, which has hosted ten mass-prayer gatherings in Canada and one in Hollywood that drew roughly three thousand believers to pray for a move of God in entertainment media. She is also the founder of 4MY Canada, an activist organization that has equipped thousands of Canadians to be a voice for socially conservative values to the Canadian Parliament. Today she and her husband, Robert, live in Los Angeles, California, and travel extensively as conference speakers and servants to various national and international initiatives. Their passion is to exhort the body of Christ to embrace all the Word of God has for them and live lives of impact. They have a particular burden to be a voice for victims of sex trafficking and coerced abortion.

A BRIGHT FLASH

By Faytene Grasseschi

W HEN I THINK about my journey with God, of all the places I've been, I'm reminded of the song "I've Been Every-where." Wherever I have been—on the streets of Vancouver, British Columbia; the mission field in Africa; or the corridors of Canada's Parliament, I have always had a brooding sense that heaven's assistance is with me.

Sometimes I have been able to connect to it very tangibly, even sense it, see it, and smell it. Other times I just "know" it's with me; it's a sense that I'm not alone. In fact, it if wasn't for the grace of God and heaven's assistance through manifestations of the angelic, I probably wouldn't be sitting here telling you these stories.

Sometimes I feel like Mr. Magoo, the nearsighted cartoon character, in the sense that the angelic are with me helping me, but I'm not even aware. I see myself sometimes in the story of Elisha and his servant, who was freaking out when they were under siege in a dangerous situation. Elisha just prayed, "Lord, open his eyes to see," and suddenly the servant saw all the angels around them fighting for them and with them (2 Kings 6:16–18).

An example of this happened recently when I was ministering at a conference. I had a real sense that God wanted to mark people for reformation and revival. From the leading of the Holy Spirit, I invited people to come forward—and a lot more came forward than what I was expecting. Pretty much the entire roomful came down! As the people came, I saw in my left periphery a flash of a massive, massive angel.

And I was so encouraged because, again as the Word says, He gives His angels who are assigned to minister to the heirs of salvation (Heb. 1:14). So I knew, as people came forward, that God had dispatched angels to be part of the commissioning moment. And it happened simply by the Holy Spirit beginning to move. By the end of the ministry time people were having encounters all across the room—without our even praying over them.

Because I had seen this flash, I told everyone, "There is an angel here right now, and some of you are going to begin experiencing direct contact with heaven. I'm not even going to lay hands on you, and you are going to feel something is commissioning you."

What was amazing to me was that later one of the pastors came up to me and said that he had seen the same angel earlier in the service. For me it was such an encouragement.

The truth is, we are all just stepping out and releasing the kingdom on earth the best we know how. Knowing that heaven's assistants are to help us, to help us release what God wants to do in different situations, that just makes it pretty fun.

THE ANGEL AT THE MALL

By Linda Breitman

O NE TIME I encountered an angel in human form. It happened early in my marriage, shortly before Christmas.

On that particular day my husband had been, well, challenging—let's put it that way. My mother was visiting, and she and my husband and I all went to the mall. It was absolutely packed with holiday shoppers, and because of the difficulty with my husband, I was nearly in tears.

I kept telling myself, "I can't cry. I'm here with my mother, and I don't want to wreck Christmas." But I am telling you, it was very difficult.

As I stood in that crowded mall with people all around me, suddenly a man was standing right in front of me. He looked at me and said, "Things are going to get better."

When he said that, I couldn't even speak. I was frozen.

I looked away to compose myself and looked back again, but he was gone. I looked around everywhere for him because the words he spoke to me were life giving. Just those few words were encouraging and uplifting and gave me hope for the future.

I didn't realize it in that moment, but he was an angel. I entertained an angel unaware!

Linda Breitman (www.LindaBreitman.com) is a frequent speaker at conferences and women's events, and an author and ordained minister. She is passionate about seeing men and women rise up in their true identities in Christ, and she is committed to mentoring the next generation of leaders. She and her husband, Les Breitman, MD, live in San Diego, California.

I FELT LOVED

By Linda Breitman

A FEW YEARS AGO I had surgery, and while I was in recovery, I was in bed and rolled over to go to sleep. Just before I fell asleep, my eyes were opened to the spirit realm.

I saw an angelic figure standing by my bed. The figure was waving his hand over my body. The immediate feeling I had was that I was being cared for, that I was being loved. I knew I was being looked after and that I was not alone. I was being healed, and my body was being restored. The angel was helping me recover from the surgery.

It all happened in a moment, and then I fell asleep. It was an awesome encounter.

ANGELS ARE BEING REACTIVATED!

By Linda Breitman

I BELIEVE THAT ANGELS are assigned to us when we are children. Children are much more sensitive to the angelic and supernatural realm than adults are. Adults often cause this sensitivity to shut down in children because when adults discount the angelic, it is shut down for children.

I have asked so many people if they saw angelic things when they were children. Many of them say they did but don't see that way anymore. Other people say they used to just "know" things when they were children—things they weren't told or things they wouldn't have had the ability or reasoning level to understand. I was like that. When I was a child, I just knew things. There is a purity and innocence in children that open them to the supernatural realm.

This ability to see or to know in that realm is being reactivated. There is a move of the Spirit now, and it is taking place for people who, as children, had supernatural giftings. They are becoming sensitive again to the angelic realm and to the fact that ministering angels are here with us all the time.

We all have these spiritual senses, but they are being reactivated now. When you get really quiet with God, you can pray: "Lord, You used to show me things, but it got shut down. I'm asking You to reactivate my spiritual senses because I want to see everything You have for me. I want to interact with everything You have for me. I want to know in my 'knower' the revelation You have for me. Lord, reactivate that in my life."

It's an awesome thing between you and God.

MASS DELIVERANCE
IN THE GLORY

By David Herzog

T HE FIRST TIME I ministered in Africa was in Gabon, a nation
on the continent's west central side. It had been an amazing
time. I preached, and the ministry was awesome.

One night when I was preaching, a woman came forward. I'll call
her "cat woman" because she was possessed by a cat-type spirit—or
the spirit thought the woman was a cat or something. But she hissed
and tried to scratch with her nails.

I was on the stage, and she was coming down closer and closer to
the front. No one intercepted her. No one stopped her—which surprised me because I expected the ministry team from Africa that I
was working with to be more used to this kind of thing than I was.
I expected them to handle it.

Also, I was a little scared because I wondered if the spirit in this
woman was a bigger principality than the people there were used
to. I wondered if that was why they weren't intercepting her. My
African friend teased me as he saw her coming, "We're just trying to
see if you white boys know how to do deliverance." But I could tell
underneath that he was a little scared too.

As she got closer, I thought about making a joke to deflect some
of the serious attention from this demon, but I was unsure how the
humor would translate. I assumed that jokes and humor would be
different there, so I didn't want to call out, "Here, kitty, kitty!" in
case I offended people. So I said nothing.

Instead I started talking to the Lord.

"What do I do, Lord? Do I stop the worship? We're almost finished with worship, and I'm on the stage and the glory is coming.
What do I do?" I knew if I stopped the glory that was falling and
began to cast out demons, then the whole service would shift and

become about that demon and that woman. I didn't want that. I knew I wasn't there for that.

The Lord said, "You have option number two"—as if option number one was to stop everything and cast out the demon. I didn't know what option number two was.

He continued, "You can do it with My angels in the glory."

I'd never done that. To me, up until that time, the glory always seemed to be more about the gifts that came with the glory and about miracles but not about casting out demons. Could I mix the glory with deliverance? It felt like I would be mixing heaven with hell.

So I asked, "Lord, how do I do that?"

"You can do it My way or your way," He answered.

As I was having this conversation with the Lord, I was thinking through with Him what my way was.

"I cast out demons in Jesus's name," I said.

"You could do that," He said, "but there is a higher way. You can do Acts 4 level and pray, 'Lord, stretch out Your hand not just to heal but to deliver'" (v. 30).

I was a little stunned, "You mean, You will deliver them?"

"Yes," He said. "If you will do it a different way, then just as you do healings in the glory without touching people, you can do deliverance in the glory with My angels."

I went for option two! In the moment, though, I almost chose option one, only because the cat woman was getting closer and closer and continuing to hiss and scratch. Part of me just wanted that demon out of there. But I waited and said, "OK, Lord, now what do I do?"

He said, "Keep singing."

So I kept singing, I kept leading the people in worship. We went into spontaneous worship, and the glory got thicker and thicker. But as the cat woman got closer and closer, I had to try really hard not to resort to the old anointing. When God brings you into a new glory, you have to press into the unknown. So I pressed in. I waited—but I thought, "Hurry, Lord. Hurry up."

Finally I began to see angels coming down from the sky into the crowd. (This was an open-air crusade, a big outdoor event.) All the while we were still singing and leading the people into spontaneous song and worship. I told the Lord, "I can see the angels. I can see them."

He told me, "Tell the people what you see. Tell them you see the angels and tell them where you see the angels."

I said, "I see an angel over here."

The people were worshipping, but they looked. They did not see it. Yet within a few seconds, hundreds of people went out on the floor, foaming at the mouth and screaming. Remember, there was a crowd in the thousands, and this began happening.

In the midst of it the Lord said, "Now look to your left," and I saw angels coming and going. He said, "Point over there where you see the angels and tell the people." So I announced, "There are angels over here." Everyone looked and immediately they started falling out in the Holy Spirit.

What followed was mass deliverance for three hours. During that time I did not get tired. I was in the glory, singing and worshipping. I was singing, "There are no demons in heaven's glory, and heaven's glory is here." The demons understood. That's right; they knew heaven was coming down and they had no authority to be there.

Deliverance in the glory is like a shortcut. It is like nuking demons instead of relying on just what you have in your own anointing. You bring all of heaven down, and you get mass deliverance. We had three hours of it. All the people were singing in the glory, but behind the scenes demons were scattering.

As all this was happening, I saw that the cat woman was now on stage. "Now what, Lord?" I thought.

He said, "She is more possessed than the other people. She has a spirit of divination. But what you need to do is very simple: ask, do not command; ask the angels to help you with healing and deliverance, and I will lead people into salvation."

So with no emotion in my voice, I announced, "Will the angels on my left and the angels on my right please accompany this woman?"

I said it just like that, only with a funny British accent for some reason.

The cat woman freaked out. She could see the angels, and she screamed, "No! Here they come! *Ahh!*"

She fell to the floor, and then flipped down off the stage, kicking and screaming. But she was completely delivered—just like that.

And because of it other people got saved. They were saved by the droves, and not just at our conference. Apparently people miles away could hear the screaming of the thousands who were being delivered, so when we made an altar call, people ran forward from everywhere to get saved—all because of a mass deliverance in the glory.

That was only my second angel experience, and it happened very shortly after my first one. It was exciting!

DANCING WITH ANGELS

By Melissa Fisher

WHILE ATTENDING a conference once, I experienced something firsthand and know it to be true: angels like to have fun with us. They like to play with us.

I learned this, I have to tell you, during a particularly hard conference. A lot of people were there, and you could feel that there was a lot of unbelief in the room. One of my responsibilities was to be in prayer and intercession, and unbelief is a big part of what intercession at a conference must combat. Intercessors are there to get anything out of the meeting room that would block what God wants to do.

After three days of it, though, I was tired. I was praying, "Lord, this is hard ground. Help us."

Well, as I was walking around outside the main conference room and rounded a corner, all of a sudden I felt hands on my waist. The hands pulled me backward and twirled me around! I turned around to see who grabbed me, but nobody was there! And I'm thinking, "OK, what just happened?"

Then the hands grabbed my waist again and pulled me backward and turned me around again. And it kept going. I was being twirled all over the place—over to the walls, down the hall, everywhere.

A friend of mine saw this whole thing and came over, laughing at me. She was pointing at me and making this crazy face because I probably looked really ridiculous. But as she walked up, she too was grabbed and pulled. So now both of us were getting turned and twirled. It was like being part of a perfectly timed dance.

We were both laughing so hard. We were having a good time. Two angels were playing with us! This was confirmed to me because somebody from across the room came over and said they saw the angels who were dancing with us. That was one of my favorite experiences! Afterward all of my heaviness was gone. The burden of praying through all that unbelief was lifted.

I know this may seem a little silly to some people, but it was exactly what I needed when I needed it. Praying and interceding for everyone else to experience breakthrough, we first had to experience that very breakthrough ourselves so that everything God was planning for the people to have while they were there could be released.

The joy of the Lord is our strength, and at that time I had lost my strength in the battle because the battle in the spirit was so hard. But the angelic experience brought such joy because there wasn't anything I could do about it while it was happening. The angels were playing around and dancing with us, and it was a lot of fun.

Sometimes we limit God by what we think that He will do and how we think He will remedy a situation. But God knew what I needed for that moment. He did it, and I could not have planned it any better on my best day.

IT'S GOING TO BE OK

By Steve Swanson

I HAVE ONE OF those angel stories that in the middle of it you don't even think about what's happening. Later, though, you think back and go, "Oh, my goodness!"

I had been suffering from an infection in my foot. I'd had three surgeries on my Achilles tendon, and then it got infected. I had to wear a medical boot for two years, and I was at my wit's end because I couldn't walk or play with my kids, and it was really painful.

The day before my fourth surgery, my wife, Lisa, had a dream in which she saw me playing with my kids again. Because of that she knew I was going to be OK. So going into this fourth surgery, we were hopeful that my foot was finally going to be all right.

As I was being prepped for surgery, an elderly woman walked in. She was sort of short, and her hair looked like a grandma's wig. Her nametag read "Glory." When I saw it, I thought that was a cool, original name.

She came over to me and said, "It is going to be OK. It is going to be OK." That was very calming and reassuring.

As the nurses were about to wheel me to the operating room, Glory winked at me. It was an "It's going to be OK" wink. I thought, "Wow, that is interesting," because she was being so nice and it made a real impression on me.

She was the last person I saw just before they gave me the anesthesia.

After surgery I remember finally becoming coherent again, and the first thing I wanted to do was find Glory and thank her for being so nice.

So Lisa and I went to the front desk and asked, "Can we speak to Glory?"

The girl at the desk answered, "We don't have anybody named Glory working here."

That is when it hit me—she had to be an angel!

No one named Glory worked at the surgery center, but she was so kind, so calming, and gave me such confidence that it was going to be OK. The realization in that moment of what had happened was awesome.

It reminded me of the account in the Bible when an angel visited Mary to announce the birth of Jesus. Basically the angel told her, "This is what is going to happen to you: You are going to give birth to this child and everything is going to be OK." (See Luke 1:30–33.)

Angels are sent to encourage us. They are sent to calm us and let us know we are protected. And we are. We are protected at all times because God cares for us. He is watching over us and sends us His angels right when we need them.

Steve Swanson is a worship leader who ministers internationally with leaders such as Patricia King, Randy Clark, Heidi Baker, Bill Johnson, and JoAnn McFatter. Since 1997 Steve and his wife, Lisa, have overseen Friends of the Bridegroom Worship Ministries (www .SteveSwanson.org), which is dedicated to the release of God's creativity in worship and the arts. He has released twenty worship CDs and continues to record and produce his own and other artists' works. He and his wife have two sons and live in Casa Grande, Arizona.

HONOR IS A KEY

By Annie Byrne

PEOPLE WHO WANT to see into the supernatural realm, who want to interact with the angelic, often wonder if there is some kind of formula, some magic pill, or something else they must do or have to see in that realm. No, none of that is right. To see in the supernatural realm does not require a magic pill, formula, or equation.

But there is something required of us. I think the best way to describe it is as "pressing in." And it involves "honor"—a key to seeing, participating, and operating in the supernatural that has been part of my journey into the supernatural.

My journey began when I visited Brazil years ago as part of a trip that happens every year called Power Invasion, in which about three hundred young Americans partner in Brazil with about three hundred young Brazilians. They pray for the sick and see God do incredible, supernatural things.

It is part of a ministry operated by a man who was healed of Down syndrome when he was eight years old. Ever since his healing, he has had a lifestyle of the supernatural. It is common for him to be taken up into heaven. He sees into the spirit realm beyond the angels and what is happening in the spiritual realm around the world. He is active in what is called the third heaven. This is what the prophet Daniel was familiar with. This man has the ability and anointing not only to see the angels but also to partner with them. He has the ability to pray an impartation for others to have this anointing as well.

His way of accessing this realm is primarily through worship. When he worships and leads others into worship, the angels come, God comes, and an atmosphere of heaven comes.

In fact, worship is one way we are able to attract angels. When you live a lifestyle of worship, in which worship is your natural state and mind-set, and you are always sowing praise into the atmosphere around you, then it creates an atmosphere that angels recognize, that they in fact like.

The Bible tells us that worship is what is happening around the throne of God, always, constantly, throughout eternity. There are lightning and flashes and signs and wonders, and angels are constantly crying out, "Holy! Holy! Holy!" The elders before the throne are constantly presenting themselves to the Lord and laying themselves out before the Lord. They are constantly throwing their crowns down before Him.

This kind of activity, this worship, creates an atmosphere of honor.

Personally, I didn't want to experience the supernatural just once or have a single encounter while away on a missions trip. I wanted to create a lifestyle of the supernatural, just like the ministry leader I mentioned. I wanted to live a lifestyle of worship and of honor.

I began doing this by creating, surrounding myself with, and being constantly engaged in prayer, praise, worship, and declarations of the Word. I purposed to create the kind of atmosphere where not only I wanted to live, but also where angels and the presence of God felt comfortable being. This is part of the honor aspect of living in the supernatural.

For example, if I were to invite royalty to my house, I wouldn't want them to come when my house was junky, dirty, and uncomfortable. I would not want them to be looking for the first opportunity to leave. I would want to honor them by making my home clean, comfortable, and enjoyable so they would want to spend time there. This is the best way I can compare creating an atmosphere of honor and worship so the angels and the actual presence of God feel comfortable and want to hang out.

Before leaving for Brazil, I spent several months reading just Revelation 4 over and over as much as I could. I was anticipating a release into the supernatural, and I wanted to be familiar in my mind and my spirit with what heaven looked like. It was my way of "seeing" heaven. Even if I couldn't see it with my own eyes, I was going to immerse myself in the Word wherever it talked about heaven. So I engrossed myself in Revelation 4. I lived in that chapter.

Revelation 4 contains the clearest picture of what is happening around the throne of God in heaven. I read it over and over, as many times as I could in an hour. I wanted to be familiar with heaven, and I thought if I devoted three months or six months or a year of my life to reading that one chapter, then it would result in my understanding heaven, and that would be worth it.

When we finally got to Brazil, we went to a meeting where the ministry leader was going to pray for everyone on the team, including me, to have our eyes opened. I was praying so hard, "I want to see. I want my eyes opened."

He prayed for the girl next to me, and her eyes were opened instantly. It was crazy! She was talking about all the things she suddenly was able to see. Then he prayed for me, but nothing happened. I couldn't see anything.

Two nights later the girl was still seeing angels—with her eyes open. She could see into the invisible realm. It was now visible to her. We would walk down the hotel hallways or into restaurants, and she would say, "There's an angel over there." So I would stop and pray, "God, let me see this angel."

I was so eager, like a kid so wanting to see these things. I didn't want to worship the angels, and I didn't want to worship the experience, but I did want to see. So badly! And we are allowed in the Bible to "eagerly desire" (1 Cor. 12:31).

The next night I was booked to preach at a church, and my friend wanted to come with me. It was only my third time to preach, ever, and I had never done any ministry or prayed for people after preaching. I was nervous.

There were about six hundred people at this church, and I knew I was supposed to go and just "let loose" and see what God wanted to do. I didn't have a message. I didn't have a formula. I was, in fact, terrified. Sometimes I think God lets us ride a roller coaster of faith so we will learn to let go and let Him just do His thing. It is all part of our partnership with Him and the angels anyway!

Before I preached, there was a time of worship, and while everyone was worshipping, I was praying, "O God, I do not want to rely on somebody else's vision or insight. I don't want to have to rely on someone else to tell me what is happening in the angelic realm. If I am going to do this, it has to be me and You doing it together. It can't be me relying on someone else."

I was sitting on the front row of the auditorium with my hands extended out. Basically I was asking God for a sign.

Suddenly I felt a raindrop on my arm. Just one drop. I began looking around. I started looking at the air conditioning vent to see if there was condensation falling. I tried to figure out if someone had opened a bottle of water. I even looked for someone with a squirt gun.

I was going through all those rational reasons in my mind trying to figure out where the raindrop came from when the Lord spoke so clearly to me, "Why are you doubting? You asked Me for a sign!"

That's when I looked down at my Bible. It was covered with raindrops. But there were not any drops anywhere else. There wasn't a puddle under my Bible, but it was covered with raindrops, splattered with water in just one place.

That was enough. I said, "OK, God, here we go. It's You and me."

In that moment I knew I didn't have to rely on anyone else to tell me where the angels were. I knew I could rely on God to reveal things to me.

But it all had begun with a process of honor—honoring the small signs and not needing the big, dramatic vision. I had to be able to say, "OK, God, You have opened my friend's eyes. I believe You can do that. I believe that what she has been telling me is truth. But You have spoken to me in this little way, and I am going to honor this sign. I will both honor her gift and partner with the gifting and anointing and breakthrough that You have put on her life, but also go in confidence with You and see what happens."

Of course, back in the church service, when I was called to the pulpit, I still didn't have a message! But it was amazing. I stood up and right away I began to feel heat and a presence behind me. The heat rose up my legs and then my back, and I knew it was from an angel behind me with fire to release. So I started sharing what the Lord was telling me, "God has sent His angels with fire to release tonight. It is the exacting justice of God, and it is going to bring healing and salvation and deliverance tonight!"

As I continued sharing and talking about the fire angel, my friend who could see the angels was on the front row, and she was laughing the whole time because what I was saying was exactly what she was seeing with her open eyes. That was how we partnered together that night. I would get a feeling, an impression, a little whisper, I would share it and my seer friend would confirm it.

I was honoring the little ways I was sensing and hearing and getting impressions. Even though I wasn't seeing the invisible things, even though there was no lightning and thunder, I was honoring the little signs I was getting. And from that small beginning, honoring the little things and small beginnings, I was able to watch the manifestations of heaven multiply and grow.

By the end of the night we had prayed for two hundred of the people there. There were twenty-seven salvations, and almost everyone we prayed healing for received healing, including a woman who was healed of a breast-cancer tumor. She went to her doctor the next day, and he confirmed that a tumor the size of a grapefruit had been reduced to the size of a pea. The doctor was astonished.

It all began with little acts of faith.

Now years later there are times when I have seen angels with my eyes open. But not very often. Sometimes I see just an outline of an angel. I have found, though, that if I settle myself in that moment and focus, then I can get clarity on the purpose of the angel and what is going on in the spirit.

I also now hear in the spirit realm, which was unexpected. When it first happened, I heard something and turned to the person next me and said, "What?" She just looked at me blankly. I asked, "Did you hear that?" And she was like, "What's *wrong* with you?"

Another time I was awakened by a knock in the middle of the night. I sat straight up, my heart pounding, freaking out. Instead of responding to it with honor and following up to see what God was trying to bring to my attention, I responded with fear.

I have learned that, as believers, we all have a choice. We can follow God either from a place of fear or from a place rooted and grounded in honor and in love. Fear will mask the encounter and make it something we strive for. But honor will open the realm of heaven.

Following God in honor will open a whole new world, a complete lifestyle of walking in God in ways you have never experienced before.

Annie Byrne is the founder and president of Momentum Ministries (www.imomentum.org). As a young girl Annie dreamed of hosting revival meetings in packed-out stadiums and seeing God move in Hollywood. After earning a master's degree in social work, Annie heard the clear and audible voice of God say to her, "I've fulfilled your dreams for your life, now I want to fulfill My dreams for your life." She spent over three years as a student and assistant of Global Awakening Ministries founder Randy Clark then joined the pastoral staff of Encourager Church in Houston, Texas. She is now a full-time traveling minister and leadership consultant.

I FELT A BREEZE
BLOWING AROUND ME

By Robert Hotchkin

M Y ENCOUNTERS WITH angels started by simply believing God's Word. God says in Psalm 91 that He will charge His angels to protect us wherever we go. That means wherever we are, angels are with us. And Psalm 34:7 says the angels of God encamp all around us. So, again, wherever we are, angels are with us.

I have a chair in my living room that I call my "prayer chair" because it is my favorite place to sit and meet with God. It's my version of Moses's tent of meeting. I sit there in the mornings, drink my tea, and talk with God. I read the Word, I study the Word, and I talk with God.

I know from my studies that the role of angels is to "minister" to us. This comes from the Greek word *diakonia*, which means to "attend, aid, serve, or wait upon as a friend." Whether we are aware of angels, whether we see them or not, this is their role, and they are all around us.

One morning as I was going through this, all of a sudden I said, "Lord, Your Word says there are angels all around me. Your Word says that angels are assigned to my life to protect me and minister to me, and even to teach me. God, I choose to believe that there are angels all around me, that they are aiding me, serving me, waiting upon me, that they are ministering to me because You say they are. God, I believe, I believe, I believe, I believe. I receive the angels of God who have been assigned to minister to me. I bless them to achieve Your purposes in my life and in the earth."

As soon as I finished praying this, so suddenly I felt a breeze blowing around me in my prayer chair. I was sitting there, and a swirl of wind was all around me, and immediately the Lord brought to mind Hebrews 1:7, which says He "makes His angels winds" (NAS).

That was it.

Simply by faith I leaned into what God says, and I accepted it by faith and declared it by faith. Then, suddenly, I started experiencing the angelic realm.

BECAUSE HE LOVES US

By Robert Hotchkin

W HEN I WAS in Eastern Europe, I ministered at some meetings in a little town called Aizkraukle, Latvia.
During a time of worship the Lord whispered to my heart, "I am going to send an angel here this morning." I was like a kid on Christmas morning. I looked all around for the angel. I couldn't wait!

I couldn't see anything angelic with my natural eyes, so I did the only thing I knew to do—ask the Lord about it.

"OK, I'm not seeing it with my open eyes," I told Him. "Will You help me sense where the angel is in the room?"

I looked all around and suddenly—not with my natural eyes but with the eyes of my spirit—I sensed where the angel was. So I asked the Lord, "What is this angel's purpose?"

"It is an angel of provision," He told me. "I am sending it to help this church, which needs provision."

That is what I heard, but I didn't say anything out loud about it for others to hear.

Instead I started preaching the message I had prepared. Then at a certain point the Lord said to me, "OK, now."

I knew it was time for me to speak with the pastor of the church. However, this was a Russian church. I don't speak Russian, and the pastor didn't speak much English. So through the translator I said, "Pastor, the Lord has told me that an angel has been sent here this morning to help you and the church."

Even though I hadn't seen the angel with my open eyes, I believed God. I believe His Word, and I believe when He speaks to our hearts. I have learned to lean into those things, even those small whispers, and to walk and act by faith; yet I am still just like a kid! I love to see God reveal Himself. Even though I know God never has to prove Himself, He loves to do it. He loves to reveal Himself to us, and He loves to reveal His kingdom.

So I told the pastor through the translator, "Start walking around, toward the back wall from where you are seated." I wanted to see if he sensed the angel was where I thought it was. If he did, it would confirm God had ordained this encounter and that what He had said to me would, in fact, take place.

The pastor started walking toward the back, and exactly when he hit the spot where I sensed the angel was, he fell to his knees and was whacked by the kingdom realm. God showed up!

The angel ministered to him, over and over and over. When he stood up, I asked him what had happened.

"I'm not really sure," he said. "I got to this one point, and I felt the reality of heaven! I feel like there was an angel right there, and I had an encounter with him."

I asked him, "Pastor, what was this angel?"

"An angel of provision," he answered.

Amazing.

What's more, for the last several years during the incredible economic crisis in Europe, this church has remained. There have been several months in which the people needed to move by faith for provision, but God always showed up.

Every single month He meets their needs, and every single month this church has more than enough. I believe a lot of this has come through the encounter with the angel Provision.

What God's angels do is incredible! All the things they do, all the things they minister to us, are incredible. But more important is why God sends them into our life.

He sends them because He loves us.

He loves us so much and wants us to become the full expression of Himself and of His kingdom. He desires us to become what He created us to be. His angels play a role in ministering to us, aiding us and helping us to become that full expression.

God loves us so much!

His angels—and His sending them—are expressions of His love for us.

PARTNERING WITH ANGELS

By Melissa Fisher

Iɴ ᴛʜᴇ Bᴏᴏᴋ of Hebrews angels are described as ministering spirits who are sent to minister to the heirs of salvation (Heb. 1:14). We are the heirs of salvation! And from what I understand— and know and have seen—there are many types of angels, and they're here to help us. They're here to serve us in our call, whatever it may be.

Sometimes they guard and protect. For example, I once was hiking down a mountain and I slipped, and I actually felt like I was picked up and let down gently. And so they're here to protect.

They're also here to serve. I've been in intercession, praying and going into really dark places, and I have asked the Lord to send His angels. They went before me to clear and pave the way.

All around us is both good and bad in the spiritual realm. When we are moving into a new area or a new territory, we can partner with God through His angels. This is true whether you are physically traveling to a place or you are going in the spirit—that is, interceding or praying into new things or new places.

That's because in the spiritual arena, a spiritual presence will occupy a place, and if it is not of God, then as we move into that place we can pray and have God send His angels ahead of us to remove the spiritual presence for us. We can go in by ourselves, but we are no match for the spiritual realm. We just are not.

But when we partner with God and His angels, God will send them ahead of us to remove whatever needs to be removed from that land or from that area. Then we can do what we have been called to do.

This is how we can partner with angels when we are doing the work and the business God has sent us to do.

I DON'T WANT TO GROW UP

By Doug Addison

THERE IS A big fear in the Christian community about worshipping angels. But the truth is, angels from the Lord won't allow it! In fact, what I have found is that when an angel first speaks to you, if you do try to worship him, then something will happen and the presence will actually start to lift, to leave.

God has sent His angels, these ministering spirits, to us to help us do the work He's called us to do. Working with them is part of working with the Holy Spirit. The Holy Spirit is like the conductor of an orchestra. He uses all the gifts. He uses all the people. He uses all the angels. He uses supernatural encounters. He uses them all together—that's called the kingdom of God. So I always encourage people not to be afraid.

The biggest thing you can learn is not to be afraid of an angel. Sometimes we fear because we had negative encounters as children—nightmares or some kind of fearful encounter. I'm convinced that this is one of the enemy's biggest ploys—get children to be afraid of the supernatural. Then we grow up with a fear of seeing an angel because as a child demons appeared in the bedroom. You know, the monster in the room at night.

We need to make the supernatural natural once again. We need to talk to our children about what they have experienced. For example, in the morning at the breakfast table ask them if they dreamed something. Ask them about these things because God *is* doing something new right now, and we are going to see a huge move, especially with our children. It will be with all types of people, but even with the children. God is using angels to interact with them and with heaven.

Children are so absolutely in tune with the supernatural. They have, I think, a faith level that we lose as we start getting older. In fact, I remember when I was a kid that adults would tell me, "You just have a wild imagination," but I really *was* seeing things in my room and would just know something about a situation.

Then as I grew up and was a young believer, I would have supernatural encounters all the time. Some of them were angelic and some were just supernatural. But people at my church would tell me: "God's just showing you that to get your attention. Later on, as you grow in your faith, you won't need that anymore"—as if encounters with God, heaven, and His angels stop with spiritual maturity.

Well, here's what I found out: I want that stuff all the time! In fact, I have had to work to go back to get it. I don't want to "grow up"—not in the sense that I would have to lose track of God's supernatural ability and my sensitivity to the Holy Spirit.

PART 4

ANGELIC PROTECTION AND ANGELS AT WAR

For He shall give His angels charge over you,
to keep you in all your ways.
—Psalm 91:11

MY GUARDIAN ANGEL LOOKS LIKE A THUG!

By Katie Souza

I WAS IN PRISON when I saw my first angel. I had been thrown into lockdown numerous times because I fought with the police and with the inmates. So there I was again, by myself in lockdown.

At the time I had only just found Jesus so I was trying to be good, but I was still acting out and having a really hard time. They told me I was going to be in there for ninety days, and lockdown in that facility was not good. It was not a private room with your own shower. I had to sleep on a little metal bench or a dirty mattress on the floor. The room was covered with urine and feces and blood, and it was freezing cold.

I was in there praying and had been praying for three days straight. I remember asking God to please come and visit me, and to forgive me, and show me favor, when I looked up and saw a huge man standing there, guarding the door of my cell. He was so big that he was hunched over; because of his size he couldn't fit in the cell standing upright.

I could see he was an angel. But his fists were balled up like he was going to beat down anybody who came into the cell. He didn't look like an angel, really; not like what you would expect. He looked more like a thug from the streets! He looked tough and all torn up, like he'd been in a huge fight!

When I saw him, I reached out to touch him, and as I stretched out my hand I closed my eyes. And then, not in my imagination but in the natural realm, my hand started going up and down like someone was shaking it, as if we were shaking hands and introducing ourselves. I could physically feel him take hold of my hand. It scared me so much I actually pulled my hand back, all freaked out.

But that was how I first met my guardian angel! Years later I was

135

being filmed for a television interview, and I met a powerful woman of God in the studio who said to me, "I can see your angels."

So I asked her, "What do they look like?"

She said, "One of them doesn't even look like an angel. He looks like a gangster, like a thug."

I got so excited. I said, "That's my angel! That's my angel!" And she said, "He's so beat up from the fight, from protecting you on the streets, that he has only one wing, and it's torn and covered with blood."

LEGION EXPERT

By Katie Souza

In Mark 5:1–20 we read a story about the demoniac, a man who was assailed by the spirit of Legion. What was it that gave the spirit the right to attack this man? It was a wound in his soul.

The Scripture tells us the man dwelled among the tombs. This man was living in a literal cemetery. The application for us is "tombs" represent the things that have happened in our past, the things that have caused wounds in our souls. In fact, the word *dwelling* in this account is a word used as a metaphor for "powers that pervade and govern the soul."

What this means is, the man was living out of the woundedness of his past; he was dwelling among the tombs. This is the way in which the spirit of Legion had the power to pervade, govern, and control his soul. The wounds in his soul gave the spirit the right to be there.

In my ministry we deal with the spirit of Legion a lot because we help people learn how to have their souls healed. The spirit of Legion is a very fierce demonic spirit. He is actually six thousand strong, and he attacks the mind and the body. We see this in the account of the demoniac where the story says that after the man was delivered from the spirit of Legion, he sat clothed and in his right mind (v. 15).

Before he was delivered, he had lost his mind. He cut himself, beat himself, bruised himself with stones, he shrieked and screamed. But after he was delivered, he had his mind back. He sat clothed and in his right mind.

I have studied this reference, and I have come to understand that to be "clothed and in one's right mind" also means to be healed of diseases. This spirit brings diseases on people. I have seen the spirit of Legion bring bacteria, viruses, flu symptoms, infections, and all kinds of diseases that have been instantly healed when people are delivered of Legion.

I remember one instance when I was in the middle of a spiritual battle and I needed help—badly. It was when I first was starting to understand how to get people's souls healed, which is to remove the spirit of Legion from them. I was asking God, "Just send me information, give me help, send me an angel—do something!" And sure enough, within about ten minutes, an angel walked into my room with his troop.

This angel looked like a Vietnam vet. He looked like a Vietnam-era Air Force pilot, complete with aviator shades, a goatee, and long hair—the whole thing. But he was wearing desert khakis, not jungle khakis—which is really interesting because there is a difference between jungle and desert khakis. All the angels in his troop were wearing desert khakis too.

The angel's name was Legion Expert. He began explaining to me a lot about Legion. He and his troop were corralling Legion and making sure they wouldn't come back to the house from which they came. When a person is delivered of Legion, these angels have a job to do. They make sure Legion does not and cannot return to that person. Legion Expert taught me how Legion works and how to battle him, how to get the souls healed, what steps need to be done, and in what order to tame this fierce beast.

Ever since that encounter with Legion Expert and his troop, we have had many meetings of mass deliverance of this spirit. This Legion spirit comes off people in large numbers, all at once, when the people's soul wounds are healed. Legion Expert and his troops show up at these mass deliverances to help remove the demonic spirits and take them out to the dry and waterless places, and to make sure they cannot return.

This is exactly what the Bible says happens. It says, "When an unclean spirit goes out of a man, he goes through dry places, seeking rest, and finds none" (Matt. 12:43).

I've seen it in the spirit when Legion Expert and his troop take these Legion spirits out, and it's pretty cool. It looks like a *Star Trek* movie when the ships go into hyper-warp drive and the light goes *woooshoo.* It looks just like that! These angels are able to travel in different dimensions. I don't know how it works, but I do know it looks just like a *Star Trek* movie effect.

How cool is that?

IT SPARKED!

By Elizabeth A. Nixon, Esq.

WHEN MY SON, Joshua, was three years old, he was playing in my bedroom while I was getting ready to go out one morning. He had taken some of my hair bands and hair clips to play with them on the floor.

I was in the adjoining master bathroom doing my hair when I smelled an acrid odor, the smell of wire burning, and heard a sizzling *zzzzzp* sound.

I ran into the bedroom and saw Joshua sitting on the floor with a very shocked look on his face. He was holding his fingers and had huge saucer eyes, although he wasn't crying. When he looked up at me, it was with one of those "Am I going to get into trouble?" looks.

I looked at the wall and saw a black mark coming out of the electrical outlet and streaking up the wall above it. The outlet itself was covered in black and a melted plastic and metal clip was in the outlet.

It was one of those awful moments as a mom when you have that sinking feeling in your stomach. In an instant you're rethinking the whole situation and already putting the blame squarely on yourself.

Running over to him, I asked, "Are you OK?"

He nodded his head but held up his fingers. I held them and kissed them, and he began to cry, more from being frightened than because his fingers hurt.

"What happened?" I asked. "Did you put one of Mummy's clips in the outlet?"

In his little quiet voice he said, "Mummy, it sparked!"

I could see the result of that spark halfway up the wall. The black mark was an awful sight. I was in shock too and really surprised that Joshua hadn't been hurt more, given the burned area on the wall and the melted clip hanging out of the outlet. In fact, I couldn't believe he had no marks on his fingers or hand and that he hadn't been shocked.

I asked him what happened.

He said, "I put your clip in there and it sparked, a big spark, and my angels did this." Then he threw himself on the bed, two feet away, and started shaking his entire body.

"What?" I said.

He said, "When the spark came out, my angels did this." And again he threw himself backward across the bed and began shaking his body.

"The angels took the shock for you?" I asked. I was trying to understand what he was telling me.

He smiled a big, laughing smile, as if it was a funny joke, and started shaking himself all over the bed. He was clearly already over any fright he'd had.

Now it was clear what he was telling me. The reason he had not been hurt from the electrical shock—which had burned up the clip and the outlet and left a blackened, burned mark halfway up the wall—was that his angels had taken the electrical shock for him!

In doing so, Joshua's angels literally were thrown two feet across the room and onto the bed, where they shook and shook from the electrical force.

I have heard of angels being physically wounded when fighting a spiritual battle for us, and I still don't understand the dynamics of how that happens. How is it that these angelic beings, who are spirit in nature, enter our natural realm and experience earthly things in their bodies?

I have to say, I don't really know how it works, but I am really glad it does. Because that morning Joshua's angels may just have saved his life!

ANGEL IN A WHITE SUIT

By Shawn Bolz

I HAVE BELIEVED IN angels since I was three years old. I believe God can interact with man and that angels and demons can interact with us too. Growing up, I didn't look for interactions, but I paid attention when they did.

When I was seventeen years old, I was babysitting two boys, Andrew and Jonathan, and I took them for a car ride. As I was starting to make a left turn, an old man who was driving too fast and wasn't paying attention hit our car.

Our car spun three times, and when it settled I heard a loud voice say, "Get the boys out of the car. You're OK." I looked next to me at Andrew, and he was OK, but the boy in the back, Jonathan, had been knocked unconscious. His seat belt was broken, and his head had gone through both the side window and the back window. He was knocked out and completely bloody.

Andrew, who was seven years old, was calling out to me, "Shawn! Shawn!" when I realized my legs were completely locked into where I was. Andrew continued, "Shawn, are we going to be OK?" and I said, "Yes, we are going to be OK, we are going to be OK"—even though at the time I had no reason to know that.

That's when a man dressed in a white suit walked up to the car. And, still, that's so funny to me because even at the end of the eighties wearing a white suit was rare. But a man in a white suit walked up to our car. He came from nowhere—I have no idea where he could have come from because no one had stopped to help us at that point. Even the old man who hit us drove off. He came back later, but at that stage there was no one else around.

The man walked over to my broken window and said, "Get out of the car. Get Jonathan and Andrew out of the car. You are all going to be OK." I felt this inner strength come inside me, and I knew that what he was saying was true.

And I said to him, "How do you know we are going to be OK though?" He said, "Trust me." And he winked, and then said, "I'll go get help."

I turned and asked Andrew, "Can you get out of the car?' He was able to get out. Then I carried Jonathan, which I knew not to do—you are not supposed to move an injured person because they could have neck or back injuries. But I had a complete assurance that Jonathan was going to be OK.

So I carried him out of the car and laid him on the grass. Not knowing what else to do, I called my parents, and then the paramedics arrived and drove us all in the ambulance to the hospital.

But here's the thing: by the time Jonathan got to the hospital there were no cuts on his body. There was only one little cut on the back of his neck, but it could not have accounted for all the blood that was everywhere in the car and on his clothes.

Now these two little boys didn't believe in God at the time of the accident; in fact, they had no grid for whether God could heal or if angels were real. Yet Andrew asked me later, "Shawn, who was that man who came up to our car?"

I didn't know Andrew had seen him—it happened so quickly that when it did even I was thinking, "This could be an angel." And he was. He was an angel.

I asked everybody who came to the scene, "Did you see this man? Did you see this man in a white suit?" But nobody saw him. He had told me he was going to a certain house to make a phone call, but the people at that house said they never saw him. Regardless, the paramedics got a call, and they came because of it.

And so, not only was I not hurt, Andrew not hurt, and Jonathan not hurt, but I was also able to get out of the car—only by a miracle. We looked at the car later, and on my side and Jonathan's side the car was so crunched up that there was no way my legs could have been pulled out. And if Jonathan had really gone through the two windows that way, since the blood was everywhere (there was a lot of blood), then there is no way I should have been able to remove him and for him to still have been OK.

That was my first experience with what I believe was an angel—an angel in a white suit.

Shawn Bolz is the founder of Expression58, a missions base and church in Los Angeles, California (www.Expression58.org). Shawn has been in ministry since 1993, speaking at conferences, in schools, and on television programs, all with a heart for training and equipping people to pursue God. He is the author of three books: The Throne Room Company, Keys to Heaven's Economy, *and* The Nonreligious Guide to Dating and Being Single. *Shawn has a burning heart to see revival in the entertainment industry and creative arts and has been influencing believers in the performing arts for many years. He currently is working on television and movie projects and lives in Los Angeles.*

ANGELS PICKED UP THAT CAR AND MOVED IT

By Joan Hunter

MANY YEARS AGO my mom and dad, Charles and Frances Hunter, wrote a book on angels. It was titled, *The Angel Book*, and filled with their own experiences with angels. Angels have always been part of my family's life.

I remember the first time Mom saw an angel. It happened during a church service, and she yelled, *"Whoa!"* because the sight of him scared her. He was a really big angel, and God told her from that encounter, "This is the angel I have promised to you, to take care of you and to protect you all the days of your life."

Angelic beings are around us a lot. I think the average person today does not realize the role angels have in our lives and the effect they have on our lives. In everyday moments like driving in traffic, when something happens and suddenly you're thinking, "There's no way I could not have just hit that car!" It missed you because an angel pushed the car out of your way.

I remember one time when I was riding in a car and all of a sudden another car was coming into our lane and I instinctively yelled, "Jesus!" All of a sudden the car went back to the other lane.

One moment it was right there in our lane, and then the next it was back in the other lane. It wasn't moving back or heading toward the other lane; it was literally as if angels picked it up and moved it, and we just kept going. And that's a key: when you call on Jesus, He releases the angels. It releases Him. It releases all kinds of things like that.

There was another time when I was going to a meeting. I was riding in the backseat, my daughter was in the passenger seat, and a third person was driving. All of a sudden a car was screeching toward us, coming directly toward the side of our car.

My daughter just moved her arm in a sideways motion. It was an instinctive reaction as if to push the car away. She didn't even cry, "Jesus!" She just moved her arm as if swiping the car away. And the car swerved away. It stopped heading toward us.

It was the angels who moved it. They redirected the other car, and we were saved from a crash!

How many times has God through His angels actually saved our lives? More times than we know!

A VISION OF WHERE I WAS GOING

By Melissa Fisher

ONE OF MY most prominent angel encounters happened once when I was just about to go to sleep. Suddenly I went into a vision. In the vision I was standing with two friends, and we were looking into the air. I saw white dots coming toward me, and it seemed as if the sky was vibrating. I looked up at the dots and saw they were Jesus and the apostles. They were all in the air. Then I started being lifted up, and I thought for a moment, "Oh, my gosh, this is the Rapture."

But as I was lifted up, I was set in front of a massive angel. It was an angel in female form, with dark hair and blue eyes, and she began to speak to me and show me different places, countries, and nations. As she was taking me around, people were beginning to follow me. I didn't understand what was happening, so I was asking, "What are you trying to tell me? What are you trying to show me?" I came to understand that she was showing me the places I would be going to.

I believe she was a messenger angel sent by God to give me a message. I also believe she was being assigned to me to do the work that she was showing me.

People do have angels assigned to them, even from birth. God assigns angels to us so we can do the work He has called us to do. In this particular situation God was calling me to be an evangelist, a harvester, and to go into various countries to evangelize.

Shortly after this encounter I did start going to places such as Thailand and Cambodia, where spiritually it's very, very dark. I went with others, and our mission was to go after sex trafficking, which is a huge demonic stronghold. I believe God gave me that angel, and maybe others, to pave the way so I could go and do that job.

At all times on these mission trips I felt the angels' presence. One way I knew it is angelic is the absence of fear. A practical example of this was when we were in Cambodia. We went to places that were full of land mines. In those places there is spiritual darkness all around, and the unexploded land mines are still everywhere. But when I go, I feel like there is always something with me. I don't have any fear.

When I talk to people and tell them what I do, I often see fear rise up in *them*. I'm often told, "I can't believe you do that!" And you know what? The danger never really occurs to me. I have this underlying sense that angels are with me, that God is with me, and so I don't have any reason to fear. It's just like when Elisha prayed to God to show his servant that there were more angels with them than there were enemies around them. I feel that way everywhere I go on assignment.

There are more heavenly angels with me than there are fallen angels with the enemy.

ANGELS GUARDING AND PROTECTING

By Melissa Fisher

A NGELS ARE HERE to guard and protect us, sometimes in dangerous places, sometimes just in everyday ways.

I encountered this protection one day while hiking. I was on a big mountain, taking a very rigorous hike. It was as much rock climbing as hiking.

While I was coming down the mountain, I stepped onto a rock and felt my feet going right out from under me. I was on a really steep section, and I should have fallen all the way down.

Instead, it was as if I fell in slow motion and somebody gently let me fall down to the ground with hardly even a bump! And I said, "Wow! That didn't hurt at all!" I just stood right back up and started going back down the mountain.

I could feel that somebody was there guarding and protecting me.

I have experienced this at other times too in my car. I have been in traffic when cars have gotten in front of me and cut me off. I should have run right into the back of them or there should have been an accident and injuries. Instead, it's almost like the whole scene slowed down so that I would be given time to keep from hitting the car in front of me.

Angels are always around to guard and protect me.

MORE WITH US THAN
AGAINST US!

By Michael Maiden

A S THE CHURCH our job is just to believe God. We are to pray,
to worship God, to declare His Word, and to unleash a tor-
rent of angelic activity because He is ready in these last days to do
everything He's ever done through history. He is ready to do it in
one compact, concentrated generation. So much of what He's ready
to do is going to be done with angelic partnerships, with their help,
support, and activity.

We are at a time in history when the angels are with us. Even
when we feel most vulnerable or weak, God is going help us. He is
going to help us come into alignment with how things really are.

Remember when Elijah's servant said to him, "What are we going
do? The enemy has come for us." And Elijah prayed, "Lord, open his
eyes." Elijah said to his servant, "Son, there are more with us than
against us." Then the same servant, who only moments before had
only seen the natural problem, discovered his eyes had been opened,
and he saw hovering over the Syrian army an angelic host of war-
riors. That took away all his fear. (See 2 Kings 6:15–17.)

The same is true for us. Sometimes our fear is based on a lack of
revelation of how things *really* are. How things really are goes like
this: *God wins!*

God is great. He has released an angelic army, and the angels
outnumber the demons. Angels are stronger than demons. Angels
are here to help us. We are on the winning team and in the winning time.

In these last days God is going to bring such an escalation of
angelic activities. It already is increasing exponentially because of
the time of history we are in. It is a tremendous time for us to really
be aware there are more with us than against us.

Whatever city you live in, whatever part of the world you live in, there are millions—countless numbers—of angels there. They are helping you, and they are helping God's purposes. They are bringing God's kingdom on earth and fulfilling God's business.

Don't be afraid. There are more with us than against us.

FROM THE TIME I WAS A LITTLE GIRL

By Stephanie Herzog

I STARTED SEEING ANGELS and demons when I was a little girl. They were as real to me as seeing the trees, cars, and houses. I was a weird child because I could see in the supernatural realm when I was so young, and no one else in my family could understand it.

My mom would invite friends and relatives over to the house for parties, and when they would come, I would not see just them; I would see all the other stuff with them. I would see demons on them if they weren't saved. I saw bunches of demons over them. If they were saved, I would see their angels, lights, and rainbows. If they were saved but struggling with something, I would see black smoke around them.

And when they would arrive, my mom and sister would say hello to the people, but I would be saying hi to the person and the whole spiritual entourage that came with them!

I got saved when I was six years old, and after that time I saw more of the angelic and the light, probably because I had the light inside me. But I still saw the demonic, which was hard because I didn't have any teaching or understanding of what I was seeing. When I realized that I wasn't like other people, it brought fear, and I would be scared. That's the reason I never watched any horror movies, because I saw that stuff all the time.

About the time I was seven or eight years old, I would go to Sunday school and to church, but it was so boring to me. Instead of sitting in the service, I would go out to the parking lot and open my Bible, and the angels and the Holy Spirit would teach me. It was awesome, and so much better than the church service! I would be out in the parking lot having a total encounter with God, being taught by Him and His Holy Spirit and the angels.

My family, however, did not have any grid or understanding for the spirit realm—let alone their daughter seeing it and being active in it. At one point they brought in a woman who was a spiritess, or something, thinking they could stop what was happening. The woman tried to cast spells over me or cast out what was happening. She took half a coconut and some oils and potions, but it didn't change anything. I still saw in the spirit.

God also revealed things to me in my dreams. They were really vivid, and I would see things that were actually happening to other people. For example, my older sister went through a rebellious phase and would not come home sometimes or not tell my parents where she was and what she was doing. My parents would worry about her.

But I would have a dream at night, and God would show me in my sleep exactly where my sister was, whom she was with, and what she was doing. I would know exactly what was going on. So I would wake up and tell my mom, and it was always accurate.

By the time I got to high school as a teenager, I was just totally on fire for God, and the spirit realm was still so real. I had grown and matured in the Holy Spirit, and God was fathering me. It produced a real burden for souls in me. I was witnessing to everyone at school, even the teachers, and I would see the Spirit of God and His desire on them.

When I would look at the people around me, I would feel His heart. There were times I was taken to heaven and shown things about a person's life. I would see whether they would be saved or not.

I was living in Chicago and would go witnessing by myself in these really bad neighborhoods. But I had no fear because I knew I had angels and their protection over me. I knew I had an entourage of angels going with me.

I would go into neighborhoods where there were drug addicts and gangsters and gunshots firing off all the time, but I had no fear. I had a focus and was too excited by seeing all these people being saved and healed.

My dad thought I was crazy! He would say things like, "Why

don't you just send money to go to people like that? Why do you have to go there? It's dangerous!" But I would tell him, "I love it!"

There were times, I'm sure, that the people I was witnessing to could see my angels. I would be witnessing to these really big guys, covered in tattoos, huge muscles, and scary looking—especially for me, a skinny little Asian girl! But these big guys would be on their knees crying and accepting Jesus in their hearts. It was because the love of God and the angels were there. Those guys were not able to be violent around that.

That alone was the intervention of the angelic.

SUPERHERO ANGELS

By Stephanie Herzog

OUR ANGELS ARE strong and mighty! That is why I don't like pictures of angels as cherubs, as baby-like children with chubby cheeks and little wings—because our angels are strong and mighty!

I remember once praying for my husband, David, and my oldest daughter when they were preparing to go to Nigeria. It was a dangerous time for them to go because there had been kidnappings and other violence, but as we were praying together at home, I instantly saw in the spirit. I told David, "No worries, honey; you have a whole bunch of angels, and they are all so different. They are going to go with you, and it is going to be awesome."

I described to him what I was seeing. These angels going with him to Nigeria were like superheroes, like the X-Men or like Fantastic Four angels! You could tell no one would want to mess with them.

One of the angels was so chiseled it made him look like he was made out of a different kind of matter, like chiseled stone. He was like Thing, one of the Fantastic Four, but not that color. He was so strong! The devil would throw darts at him, but they would just bounce off. He looked so fierce and mighty and scary.

There was another angel who looked like a human torch! The flames of fire were from heaven, and he was made of these flames.

Other angels looked like they had weapons built right into their bodies. They were so *not* like the quiet, white-robed angels we see in pictures, with blond hair and nice wings. They can look so different!

And they are purposed to do God's bidding for us and to work with us.

THE MILITARY ANGEL

By Pam Wright

M Y SON, JOSEPH, was fifteen years old in 2001 when 9/11 happened. It was like a clarion call for him to join the military. We found out later that it was a call to so many young men. In that sense it really backfired on Osama bin Laden because his actions called a whole generation and galvanized them to defend us.

So our fifteen-year-old son began talking about the military from that point on. Although we were proud of him to have this response, it weighed very heavily on our hearts.

When Joe turned nineteen, he said, "Mom, Dad, I'm gonna go in." He wanted to join the Army and specifically be a Ranger, which is like the SEALs in the Navy. My husband and I fasted and prayed. We prayed first for the Lord to change his heart because we were devastated about it. We knew to trust the Lord, but it is a fearful thing to send your son into the Army.

Our son also fasted. He fasted for seven days. When he was done, we knew he had heard from the Lord and that he was to go in. So he did. He entered training for the Army Rangers, and it was quite extensive and rigorous. We knew that whether he made it into the Rangers or qualified only as an Army regular, he would be deployed either way.

Around this same time we invited a speaker to our church. My husband, Rick Wright, and I pastor together in Los Angeles, and the speaker we asked to come has a ministry to teach Christians to open their spiritual senses to the spiritual realm, to the angelic realm. During the meeting at our church this man said we were to pray in the Spirit and walk around the room and see if we could discern whether there was an angel in the room. He said this because he knew angels were there.

So I began walking around the room praying in tongues. I had never had an encounter with an angel before. I had never seen one, and even though I was excited to try it, it wasn't like I was full of faith for it. I was simply thinking, "I'm going to do this because I respect the man who is teaching us." As I prayed and walked around the room, I just suddenly sensed that in the corner where I was standing there was another presence. I was encountering a presence.

This was all by impression. I did not see the angel with my natural eyes, only with my spiritual eyes, through an impression. I was just suddenly alerted. As I stood there, the minister came over and confirmed that, yes, there was an angel in that corner. He told me to test, or to discern, the spirit and then he walked away. I said out loud, "Do you believe that Jesus came in the flesh, and do you believe that He is the Son of God?"

Instantly I knew that this angel saluted me and said, "Yes, ma'am."

It was a very military-like response. It was the way soldiers in the military always say "Yes, ma'am" or "No, ma'am." This angel saluted and said, "Yes, ma'am." He was tall, really tall, and he continued, "I am going with your son to Iraq."

When he said that, it was an arrow to my heart. It pierced my heart.

That is all he said, but in that answer I also knew he was saying, "I will not leave him. I will be with him. I will protect him." I heard it all in my spirit, like a knowing, even though all the angel said was, "I am going with your son to Iraq."

I walked over to my chair and sat down, stunned. Then the tears flowed, like water, like from a tap the tears ran out of my eyes. I told my husband about the encounter, because Joe had qualified and become a Ranger. He was set to deploy, and we didn't know where, but the angel had told me, "I am going with your son to Iraq."

We both sat there quietly weeping, and then the peace came over me. I had never felt that peace until that moment, until the encounter with the angel.

Over the years our son served as an Army Ranger. He deployed three times, twice to Iraq and once to Afghanistan. He was on very intense missions; most of it was classified, and he was not allowed to discuss it with us. We never knew where he was. He told us later he sometimes did night missions and that he worked many missions with Seal Team 6, the unit that took out bin Laden.

Every time he would deploy, I would pray, and I knew the angel was with him. Joe has been out of the Army for four years, but even to this day I can be overcome with emotion and fall on my knees to thank the Lord, and thank His angel, for the sovereign protection they gave my son. I am sure the angel is still with Joe, watching over him.

This encounter stayed with us for the entire four and a half years that Joe was actively being deployed, during three very intense deployments, very intense missions. Through it all we knew this angel never left him; he never left our son's side.

We are so grateful.

Pam Wright and her husband, Rick, are the founders and senior pastors of The Gathering Place (www.GatheringPlace.us) in North Hollywood, California, a church plant of Harvest Rock Church in Pasadena, California. Rick and Pam have one son who is an Army Ranger and two daughters.

A TERRITORIAL SPIRIT

By Pam Crowder-Archibald

S EVERAL MONTHS AGO I was scheduled to do a ministry event in the West Valley of Phoenix, Arizona. I had been asked by a pastor to come and do some deliverance ministry at his church, so the plan was to do just that—cast out demons. The night before the event I had prepared and was ready to go. I went to bed to get some rest.

That's when I had a visitation from an evil spirit. It came and was in a rage! It was carrying on and on, so I began to rebuke it. I was engaged in spiritual warfare, but I didn't really know what was going on or what it was about. I bound it, rebuked it, and applied the blood of Jesus—all the stuff you're supposed to do in warfare. Finally the spirit left, but I was like, "Wow!" because the warfare had gone on for two or three hours.

The next day my assistants and armor bearers and I headed over to the West Valley for the ministry engagement. I am telling you, the Holy Spirit showed up, and there was amazing ministry! It was a powerful event.

Afterward I asked the Lord, "Who was that spirit, and why did he show up?" And the Lord told me, "That was the spirit of the West Gate. He is a territorial spirit that did not want you to come and minister deliverance on the west side of town because he is the gatekeeper of that region. You were invited by a pastor in that region, you had authority, and the protocols all were in order, but that demonic entity was over that region where the church is, and it did not want you to come and minister deliverance."

Since that deliverance-ministry event, and because there was such breakthrough, that church has actually continued to go through a lot of spiritual warfare. In fact, I gave them a prophetic word that they really have to do this warfare. They have to do it—and then breakthrough would come.

When I got home from that event, I went to bed. That's when God's holy angel showed up. He was a huge, huge angel. He was not just tall; he looked like the movie character the Hulk, except he was not green, and he looked better, much more light. But he was beefed up.

His presence was powerful! Actually it was funny, because every angel has a personality. This Hulk angel came in while I was in bed, and he looked at me as if he was just there to "check in" and make sure that I was OK. I had a sense that nothing was going to happen to me that night. No evil spirit was going to show up. Then he left. And that was it.

The Lord sent that angel to let me know, "It's OK. I've got your back. You are not going to have an encounter with that evil spirit again. You have done your assignment, and you are protected."

A FULL MOON

By Steven Springer

O NE EVENING I was praying in my room; it was during a full moon, and I could feel an intensity in the spirit realm. At one point the Lord caught me up in the Spirit, and as He did, I was taken by a host of angels over a witch coven that was in the process of doing incantations in a cemetery. It was a place I had never been to, but when I went there in the Spirit, I knew exactly where I was.

I was with the Lord and His angelic hosts, and He asked me to begin to release by faith the reality of His kingdom, to call down His kingdom so that where the words of the incantations meant to bring harm there would instead be life and Spirit released.

The angelic hosts were so cool because they surrounded the whole thing. There I was, over this coven, and the angels surrounded both the witches and me over them.

Then, as the dark spirits tried to penetrate, the angelic hosts just held their ground. It was as if there was an attitude among them of, "Nope, you are not going to mess with this one [me] because this is about a greater reality that you are not going to stop."

I woke up the next day, and I knew I had to go to this community. It was actually not too far from where I lived. So I drove over there, and as soon as I arrived, I knew this was the place I had been in the Spirit the night before.

For me partnering with heaven like this has been so natural. It's part of my journey, and even members of my family have similar experiences.

I believe this is the real way God wants us to live; He wants us to partner with heaven as a normal part of our life. The Word tells us that angels are sent to assist those who will inherit salvation. That's us. The angels are looking for a good time! They are looking for us to partner with them. And I do not want my angels to be bored!

SEEING BEYOND THE VEIL

By Steven Springer

I WAS ATTENDING A meeting in Chicago when a guy began to pray or really just to call out: "Father, send Your angels! Send Your angels! Send Your angels!" In that moment I felt a presence literally lie on my shoulders.

I turned and looked both ways to see what was going on, but nobody was there, and there wasn't anything on my shoulders, not in the physical realm anyway. So I asked the Lord, "Who is it?" Then an angel came around and stood in front of me and said, "I am Ephraim. I am your angel." He continued, "Put out your hands." So I put out my hands, and he put a massive sword in my hand.

I researched the name Ephraim, and it means "a double portion" or "double fruitfulness." Ephraim is still always with me, and he has lots of angelic friends who are always hanging around too. He is a warring angel, and I am able to partner with him through my prayers and the Word. Together we bring down darkness.

That's what we all are supposed to do, and it is the fun part that God allows us to share in, to partner in. These angels are around God's throne all the time, and with open eyes we can see them around us all the time too. I have prayed this over other people a lot—for them to be able to see in the angelic realm. I believe it is an aspect of the gift of discernment, to be able to see and know what is happening in the spiritual realm.

It is exactly what happened in the Bible when Elisha prayed that the eyes of his servant would be opened to see "the reality" of the angels around them. I believe that as a prayer of faith is prayed, people many times are opened up to the realm of the Spirit. Whether that means seeing angels or whether it is just a "knowing" of things in the atmosphere that goes beyond our explanation, both are ways of "seeing beyond the veil."

DARKNESS FLEES

By Steven Springer

WHEN I SEE something in the spirit, I ask the Lord, "Why am I seeing this?" Many times we see things and God doesn't actually want us to do anything about it. He just wants us to be aware that this is reality, that this is the true reality. But at other times He says, "Oh, and by the way, bind that one." You do, and in a moment you see darkness taken down.

For example, I was driving on the highway one time, and that very thing happened. The heavens were instantly opened, and I saw a massive territorial spirit over southern Wisconsin and northern Illinois. The Lord said, "Bind him!"

Now I have to say, that is not something I do every day! But it was clearly an order from the Father, and as I obeyed, tentacles coming off that spirit began to snap off. The Lord said, "Oh, and by the way, it is going to appear as if things are getting worse because he is afraid. He knows he is losing his grip."

The very next day I saw it again, and I asked the Father, "What do I do?" He told me exactly what to do. And that's the wisdom God wants us to function in. The Word tells us that Jesus did only what He saw the Father doing and said only what the Father was saying. So sometimes we may see things in the spirit realm, but there may not be a need for us to go out with warfare. Sometimes we just need to wait for the command of the Father.

For example, I was at the church prayer room one night, and a group of us were worshipping and praying. A man came in, and it was obvious he was intoxicated. You could smell the liquor on his breath, and his behavior was manifesting in ways that there was obviously some evil spiritual stuff going on.

I went over to him and began a simple conversation with him. At one point I said, "I really feel like I'm supposed to pray for you." We went together into one of the church's small prayer rooms, but as I was praying for him, he got out of his chair, grabbed me by the throat, and began squeezing and squeezing and squeezing my neck to the point that I could hardly breath.

I reached up and gently grabbed his hand. I squeezed it and said, "You can't kill a dead man. It is no longer I who lives, but Christ lives within me."

With that this guy instantly sat down. He was growling, "Grrr, grrr." He jumped up a second time to try to hurt me, but I said, "Do you see the angel behind me?"

All of a sudden he got down on his knees, so I started praying, "Father, would You send more of these angels?" The next moment the whole room was full of angels, and this guy was curled up on the floor in a fetal position, crying and screaming. The demons in him were calling out audibly: "No, no, no, no, don't hurt us! Don't hurt us! Don't hurt us!" Over and over and over again they were calling out.

We prayed for this man. We partnered with heaven, and when we asked the Father to send His angels, He did. He is always willing to.

In the case of this man, he did receive some deliverance that night, but he wasn't fully delivered. There is stuff still going on with him, but the purpose of that night was for him to see the truth. He was able to see the reality of the angelic and the truth that demons no longer have to hold him. It was for his sake that he got to see we have authority in Jesus to set people free. He saw that when the angels of light come, the true angels of light, the darkness flees.

WAITING FOR SOMEONE TO PRAY

By Steven Springer

O NE NIGHT MY wife and I were with some friends, about a dozen of us, worshipping and praying. We had come together because of one couple who were experiencing tremendous spiritual warfare. They were seeing some really demonic stuff. So during this time we were all in prayer together for them, to really pray over them.

All of sudden, in a single moment, *bam!* I and one other guy were taken up in the Spirit!

It was unique because we all experienced it together. This other guy and I were in the Spirit together, seeing the same things at the same time. Everyone else in the room could hear our voices describing what was going on because our bodies were still there in the room. But our spirits had been taken to another realm, and we were with God the Father.

In that realm we were able to take a survey of what was happening on the dark side around the family we had gathered to pray for. We were able to see exactly what was going on, and we called out, "God! Send Your angels!" Then *whoomp*—like a flash of lightning, as far as our eyes could see, angelic hosts started showing up. They were warring angels. I mean, they were buff angels with massive swords, and their armor was polished so brightly that it was almost white.

One angel stepped forward and said, "We have been waiting for someone to pray." My only response was, "*Whoa!*"

This angel resumed his position, and the host of angels went off, and all of a sudden we could see a war taking place. We were able to watch this war between the angelic of God and the dark spirits. It was a literal war, taking place in the heavenlies. We watched it go on for several minutes over this family's house and their neighborhood. We couldn't believe it; it was so real. It was *real*.

As I thought about it afterward, it brought to mind what Paul wrote in 1 Thessalonians 5:17, "Pray without ceasing." We don't know what our prayers actually are activating!

That evening I got to see a reality of what happens when we pray. I saw that, as we prayed and asked the Father to release His angels on behalf of this family—on behalf of what was going on, against the way of darkness—we were able to actually see the hosts of heaven come in and just explode and erupt over that family and their home and their entire household.

The reality of what I saw was more real than the reality of what you and I live in every day.

WARRING WITH ANGELS

By Rene Springer

I ONCE HAD AN angelic experience during a prayer meeting that would forever change my view of angels and how they function. A group of us had gathered to specifically pray for a couple who had been experiencing paranormal, demonic activity in the house they rented. The couple was not with us for the prayer meeting but had told us previously: "The woman from whom we are renting a room also lives in the house and stays in her room all the time and rarely comes out. She keeps the lights on all night, and the TV is going all through the night. There is something not right. There is also one room that this woman keeps shut and locked all the time. One day when she wasn't at home, we got into the room, and it was completely destroyed. Everything in there was messed up, and there is a really foul smell coming from that room."

The final strange phenomenon that made them come and ask for prayer was seeing an image of a small child in a window once as they were leaving the house. Since there were no children living in the house, this image freaked them out.

The things they told us sounded like scenes from a horror movie, but they insisted, "This stuff is so real, and we don't know what to do, but we know that you guys have encountered this kind of thing before and we need help."

So we gathered a group to pray for them. As we were praying, my husband, Steven, and another man, were taken up in the Spirit. They shared a joint supernatural experience.

All of a sudden they both said, "I'm leaving my body." They saw each other in the Spirit, and both were taken together. The rest of us continued to pray while they were physically seeing the spiritual activity that was happening as we continued to pray.

They told us what they were seeing in the Spirit; it was like a motion picture was playing out right in front of them. They could see the demonic activity actually happening over the rental house. One of the things they saw was a demonic symbol that was centered around that house. Those of us in the room praying heard them ask God to send His angels. They expressed their amazement as they saw hundreds of massive warring angels come forth from heaven and stand at attention saying, "We have been waiting for someone to call us forth." They went on to describe the demons they were seeing as imps while the angels were massive. As we heard what they described, we continued to pray into it with great vigor. We knew that things were taking place in the spirit as we agreed with heaven's agenda in prayer. Heaven's angels were taking out the demonic imps with great power and ease as the two of them proclaimed heaven's victory.

At one point they asked for Jesus's cross to come and cover the demonic symbol over the neighborhood. They then actually saw a gold cross come up from the ground, and as it did, the satanic symbol shot upward as if it was repelled away from the house by the cross.

After the house was spiritually cleansed, Steven and the other man came back from this shared vision. All of us in the prayer room were marveling at what just took place. We all knew there had been a great victory as the heavenly hosts cleaned house.

Right after this, we called the couple on the phone and asked if we could go in the house with them. We knew some things had happened in the spirit realm, so we wanted to confirm it in the natural.

We arrived at the house, and the couple came running out. They were freaking out—but in a good way! They told us, "Everything is different. Everything, you know, just seems different. People in the neighborhood were out walking and that rarely happened."

We went into the house and up to the room where the stench was coming from, and it no longer smelled. The foul smell was completely gone. Then we went to the room the woman had always locked herself into. She came out and looked at us and hugged everyone. She knew something had happened. Everything had changed. She knew that the house was now clean, spiritually.

This woman had been bound by the demons that inhabited

that house, but God came in with His angels and did some house-cleaning! And we all got to co-labor with His work as we prayed!

This experience forever changed my prayer life and the limited view I had on the function of angels. I now realize when prayers of faith are released, they activate the angelic host to war and move on behalf of those being prayed for. They are waiting for us to pray and call them forth!

Rene Springer and her husband, Steven, are the senior leaders of Global Presence Ministries (www.GlobalPresence.com), an apostolic ministry based in Madison, Wisconsin. Part of the Apostolic Council of Prophetic Elders, Steven and Rene have seen thousands of people saved, delivered, and healed as they have ministered throughout the United States and internationally in countries such as Ghana, Uganda, India, Israel, Italy, and Russia.

I CAN FEEL THE ANGELS

By Elizabeth Springer

I AM TWELVE YEARS old, but even since the time when I was really young I have been a "feeler." I don't really *see* angels, but I can feel them. I can feel whether a presence is a spirit or an angel and whether it is good or bad.

My parents have raised me like this. They have taught me to know the angelic. My friends have been raised the same way. It's really cool. I like it because all my friends are spiritual, and we all experience different angelic things, both good and bad. So, yeah, we like to hang out and experience these things together. It's cool!

People who are "seers" see angels either with their eyes or in the Spirit. As a "feeler" I usually have this thing I do—I can put my hand where the angel is and then I feel a tingling, or a sensation like that, in my hand.

It feels different for different types of angels. What I feel depends on what angel is there. I may feel a tingling, or fire, the fire of God; or I have felt the angel of comfort. There are all sorts of different angels I can feel.

When the demonic spirits are around, I will feel it. Like, suddenly, I may get irritated or suddenly get sad or feel some other emotion, maybe just start feeling weird. And usually it will happen all of a sudden, either when I walk into a room or when I am talking to someone and suddenly I pick up on how that person feels or I suddenly pick up on something demonic that has come into the atmosphere.

Well, one day I was hanging out with a couple of friends, and we were just playing and hanging out in the front yard when all of a sudden we all felt an evil presence. It was like we all were suddenly scared—it was not a good feeling! So we went inside and grabbed our Bibles and some flags for worshipping and went back outside to pray and sing worship songs, read the Bible together, and dance with the worship flags.

So we did that—like we have been taught to do—and we felt that demonic presence leave, and then we felt a good presence come. One of my friends, who is a seer, said he could see different angels come into the yard. So I put my hands where he would see the angel, and I could feel the tingling and different sensations on my hand. Then I would move my hand, take it away from where he said the angel was, and the sensation would stop. I would just feel normal again.

It was so awesome that we went back inside and got the adults. We were telling them, "You have to come check this out!" So the adults came outside, and they felt the angels too. We all were like, "*Whoa*, this is awesome!"

And then we started going around the yard to feel where different angels were. They each had different sensations, and they also had different fragrances. Each angel had a different smell and a different sensation or presence. One had the fire of God and had a hot-cinnamon smell. Another one was a comfort angel, and you could just feel God's comfort come all over you, His delight over you.

It was really cool. We just kept touching the angels like that. It was an amazing encounter for all of us.

Elizabeth Springer is the twelve-year-old daughter of Steven and Rene Springer, the senior leaders of Global Presence Ministries, an apostolic ministry based in Madison, Wisconsin.

THE SCISSORHANDS ANGEL

By Annie Byrne

ONCE WHEN I was in Brazil, I was scheduled to minister at a church, and the pastor, his leaders, and my ministry team had come together to pray before the service. This was before I was really able to see in the spirit realm. It all was pretty new to me.

After we finished praying, one of the girls with me, who was able to see into the invisible realm with her natural eyes, told me, "When you were praying, angels came into the room. In fact, there is one standing behind you now. He's the biggest angel, and he doesn't really have hands; he has swords—like Edward Scissorhands (the movie character who had scissors for hands). This angel has swords for hands."

I'm not really sure why the angel had swords for hands! But there are other unusual things like this described in the Bible. For example, in the Book of Revelation there is a reference to Jesus in heaven having a double-edged sword coming out of His mouth (Rev. 1:16). The Bible has references to swords of justice and swords of righteousness. There are swords that "rightly divide," there are swords that give life, and there are the dual natures of God.

Although I don't know specifically from the Bible about swords for hands, I do know this for sure: we are talking about things that exist in a supernatural realm, and sometimes there is nothing on earth like the things in the heavens. So, like John the Revelator, we create images and analogies as best as we can to describe supernatural things in natural terms.

FOCUS ON THE
KINGDOM OF GOD

By Doug Addison

W HEN I WAS in the occult, I was operating in the demonic
realm. I had a spirit guide that was very similar to a guardian
angel or a guiding angel like believers have. Now, I completely separated from this spirit guide back in 1988 when I discovered what
it was, that it was in fact demonic. But it worked very similarly to
angels.

That's the interesting thing. Satan copies everything God does.
Satan is a created being. He was created by God, but he himself is
unable to create. He can only counterfeit or distort what God does.
So in that sense Satan and the demonic realm work very similarly to
the way the Holy Spirit and God work.

I think people put way too much emphasis on the demonic.
When people find out I was in the occult, they want me to come
and tell them what Satan is doing in their town. They want to know
the different levels of darkness. I usually tell them, "Hey, we can
settle this right now. You don't even need to pay me to come and tell
you what's going on. Here it is: Satan is lying, cheating, and stealing.
What more do you need to know?"

Isn't it much better to know what God is doing? Because that is
what counts! Yes, it's nice to know a strategy of the enemy. But the
truth is, if we focus more on God, on the Holy Spirit, on the angels,
on the love of Jesus—if we focus more on those things—then the
demonic just loses its power over us!

PART 5

ANGELS IN WORSHIP

Then I looked, and I heard the voice of many angels around the throne, the living creatures, and the elders; and the number of them was ten thousand times ten thousand, and thousands of thousands, saying with a loud voice: "Worthy is the Lamb who was slain to receive power and riches and wisdom, and strength and honor and glory and blessing!" And every creature which is in heaven and on the earth and under the earth and such as are in the sea, and all that are in them, I heard saying: "Blessing and honor and glory and power be to Him who sits on the throne, and to the Lamb, forever and ever!" Then the four living creatures said, "Amen!" And the twenty-four elders fell down and worshiped Him who lives forever and ever.
—Revelation 5:11–14

SEEING ANGELS THROUGH A CHILD'S EYES

By Joshua Mills

WHEN I WAS a little child in kindergarten, I remember sitting in church with one of my friends, and we'd see angels fly around the sanctuary. This happened for several weeks. We would just sit there and talk about it back and forth together about how these angels we both could see were flying around. It was just so real. It was normal for us—we heard about angels in the Bible, and we would see them in the church.

So one day we shared about this with some adults in the church. Their response was, "You can't see angels. You're not able to see angels. That's impossible. You're making up stories."

And in that moment something happened, and all of a sudden a door shut off. A door came down and stopped all that from happening in my life. I never saw the angels in church again. I didn't see them anywhere, in fact, and I wasn't even aware of that realm any longer. And it was because people told me that it wasn't real.

What's amazing to me now as an adult is that the Bible doesn't say we are to come to God with faith like a sophisticated intellectual or like a well-educated individual. The Bible says we come to Him with faith like a little child (Luke 18:17).

Looking back on the situation, I realize that when I was a child, because I had heard what the Bible said and believed it, I was open to see in the spirit realm. It was so easy. I wasn't trying to make it happen. I wasn't striving. It just happened. My friend and I just saw the angels flying around in church. In fact, I didn't even ask to see the angelic. It just happened naturally.

But when other people got involved and began telling me what God can and cannot do, or will not do, the encounters stopped. When they told me what I should not be seeing, that shut it off for me.

It wasn't until years later, when I was at Ruth Heflin's ministry, that the whole realm was reactivated in my life and opened up again. Ruth was a Pentecostal evangelist and revivalist. I was at her Calvary Pentecostal Campground when I began asking, "God, every kind of anointing, every kind of gift, every kind of spiritual blessing that is in this place that nobody else wants to receive, I want to receive it. Those things that are just lying dormant in this place, God, I just want to receive all of it."

I went to bed that night and had a dream. I saw three angels; they came to me, and when they did, I asked them their names. They told me their names, and in fact they told me they were my guardian angels and that they had been assigned over my life. They proceeded to tell me all the different things they had been assigned to do.

That marked the beginning, once again, of my being familiar with the angelic realm.

Since then God has taken me into the Word and shown me hundreds of scriptures detailing all kinds of encounters with the angelic realm, about how angels encounter mankind and how they interact with us.

God has even given me three keys for how I can activate the angelic realm in my life and how other believers can activate the angelic in their lives. It has been so powerful because, as I minister in that way, many people find themselves being activated in the angelic realm too.

The activation of the angelic realm is not for self-glory. It's not for self-promotion. It's not so we can say we're more spiritual than somebody else. The reason God sends angels to mankind, the reason God sends angels into the earth, is for interaction with mankind. It is for interaction with humanity so that the purposes of heaven can be released.

Ultimately the purpose of the angelic realm interacting with mankind is so Jesus Christ will be glorified in the earth.

JOY ANGELS

By Georgian Banov

THERE ARE A lot of joy angels around me. When I play my violin, they love it. There is something about it—I have no idea what it is—but they like it. When I start playing the violin, they call their friends, and then many more angels come. It is just amazing. They dance, and sometimes they imitate me with my violin bow going back and forth.

The angels dance in a whirlwind, a whirlwind of real joy.

There are different angels for different functions. The angels around me, especially when I play the violin, are joy angels. There are also messenger or announcement angels, like the ones that announced to the shepherds in Bethlehem, "Joy to the world." These are not just any angels; they are especially for those proclamations. They make the announcements about the things of the Lord. They release the joy of the Lord.

Those are the kinds of angels who hang around with me.

Georgian and Winnie Banov lead Global Celebration (www .GlobalCelebration.com) through which they hold apostolic renewal meetings and conferences worldwide and lead people into God's presence with their exuberant praise and deep, intimate worship. Filled with compassion for the poorest of the poor, they host "kingdom celebration feasts"—lavish evangelistic feeding crusades—throughout the developing world. Although the sounds, flavors, and spices of these feasts vary from nation to nation, they find God's extravagant love in each place is always the same: deep, passionate, all-consuming, and irresistible.

ANGELS AROUND
THE THRONE

By Georgian Banov

I HAVE MY OWN collection of angel stories because since I was
born again, I have had interactions with angels. My first expo-
sure to angels was when I had my first trip to heaven. When I saw
the Lord, He was covered with angels.

I saw the throne, and it was covered with a myriad of angels who
were in ecstasy. They were so close to God that they were being radiated with His love. Their reaction to it was as if they couldn't handle
it. There was too much love. The love of God being radiated on them
was overwhelming them.

I think believers have the idea that when we are in heaven we
are going to get used to God's love, that in eternity we will get used
to being exposed to it. No! God's love is an ever-increasing experience, and I was seeing that even the angels themselves are overwhelmed by it. You would think that because these angels have been
around God all this time, since the beginning of creation, that they
would be used to it, but there are levels and levels of His love that
He reveals and releases to them.

What I saw was like an overdose, a moment in which the angels
experienced an overdose of His love and His pleasure. The Bible
says, "In Your presence is fullness of joy; at your right hand are plea-
sures forevermore" (Ps. 16:11).

That is what I saw. I saw them in an ecstatic experience of pleasure from the Lord.

That was my first visual encounter with angels.

And it was then that the fire of God started falling through
them onto me. It was like constant flashes of lightning and fireballs
coming out of God. He just emanates love, so fire came on me, and

that is how I was touched by the personal fire of God—His love, the Holy Spirit, His fire.

From that point on I have had different incidents with angels.

A DANCE FLOOR IN
THE THRONE ROOM

By Georgian Banov

ONCE I WAS in Washington State to minister at a Foursquare church. The pastor picked me up at the airport, and as we were on our way to lunch, he was exceptionally eager and excited. He said to me, "Something wonderful will happen, and I know that you carry something that I want, something that I need. So I am going to get it from you!"

I love that. I love that exceptional extra hunger! So I shared with him different things that I know, things the Lord was showing me, and he was drinking it in.

That evening in the service the band, the pastor, and his worship team were totally ready and full of expectancy. They had all the music and charts ready. They were totally prepared, keyed up, and ready to go.

We started the service, and it went great. As usual there was a wonderful spirit and atmosphere. We broke into joy, which for me is one of the secret key elements I wait for; I wait for a supernatural joy to break out in the service. Joy is a spiritual frequency the demonic cannot stand. They cannot sustain themselves in it. It has a crippling and maddening effect on them. Satan does not like to be mocked, so laughter is the last thing he wants to hear from us. So joy is a very, very powerful element, and I always aim to break into the level of joy at which it breaks out and the heavens are released. Heaven is full of joy! I want to connect with that joy.

The joy in the service that night was great. It really exploded and peaked, and from that point on it was just flowing. And then during one of the worship songs I had an unusual experience.

One moment I was playing the guitar and leading the band right behind me, then all of a sudden, *whoosh!* We were right in the center of the throne room.

I have seen different aspects of the throne room, but this time it had a dance floor, like a circle or a square area. And it had a focal point—a center of attention of worship right before God. All of a sudden it was me and the band and the entire group of people on this dance floor in the center of the throne room.

The church group that night wasn't very big, but it was very united. And *boom*, there we were as clear as a bell, in the throne room. I was even aware of the spotlight—the visual spotlight of God's attention.

But it wasn't just God's attention. All the angelic were also looking on, and there were also people there, like the cloud of witnesses, all the saints before us. I don't know whether they were special or who or what they were, but there were clouds of witnesses as an audience—a human audience as well as an angelic audience.

They were in what appeared to be theater balconies, like in a ballet theater that has round, private balconies for special guests with room for just one or two people to sit in very close to the stage. It is like they are so close they can touch the performers.

So this was like endless rows of balconies, yet every balcony was close within reach. Every seat was a front seat. I don't know how, but that's how it was, that's how it felt. I was seeing millions of the angelic and clouds of witnesses, people, watching. But yet they were all still within reach even though there were towers of balconies.

There I was in the center of the throne room, and I was leading worship straight to God. I was becoming conscious of the fact that I was the focal point, and all these angels and the human audience were cheering, "Hurray, you made it!" It was as if we had made it to this focal point where they could see us because we had broken through whatever layers there are between earth and heaven. We had broken through. And it was a corporate thing because I could feel that the band was with me, even the people in the church. It was like a corporate breaking through, and all of us were right there together.

This vision lasted probably twenty to thirty seconds at the very most. It was there, and then just began to fizzle away, and I lost sight of it. Then we were back in our church down here.

Later that night we kept hearing testimony after testimony from the congregation that they had seen visions. It was a phenomenal night for everybody, but for me it was being at the focal point of worship that was so amazing. I meditated on it and talked to the Lord later about it, and He told me that there is always somebody, a singular person, who is there and who is the focal point.

Some people may go to heaven and stay just a minute or two, others a second or two. In my case it was twenty to thirty seconds, and then I phased out. But then someone else came into the throne room dance floor. There is always somebody from earth breaking through into these heavenly places, and there is always somebody from earth visually worshipping before the throne.

Who? I don't know. How did I get there? How does somebody else get there after me or before me? I don't know. It's almost like the Spirit is brooding over the body of Christ globally. He interacts with us and with just the right elements.

Some people may want to know the formula. How do you make that happen? How can you get to the throne room and onto that dance floor? I don't know about a formula. I do know that the pastor was very hungry for an experience with the Lord, and he was expectant that he would receive something from me. The band was very eager and very prepared. The whole congregation, though not very big, was tight and together and focused on that event.

A year later we repeated the event but this time with a bigger conference style. Other worship leaders were invited, and it was a phenomenal time, but nothing like what happened the first time.

But it did happen the first time, and I've asked the Lord, "What is it?" He has told me it was a sum total of the hunger and expectancy, the faith level and also the childlike purity, and the wonder of God. And because the people were ready for it, there came a moment when we were so together, in one accord because of all those components and elements, that it just clicked and we broke through.

There is a point of breakthrough at which everything reaches a certain point and then, *boom*, you're just there.

The point is, it can happen, does happen, and there is always somebody there. There will always be those who break through. The Lord has said there will always be one person. It could be a worshipper in Tibet or someone in their closet worshipping the Lord. Yet, just like that, he or she is right there. It could last for a moment; it could last for an hour. But it is a supernatural thing.

And it's a phenomenal thing. It is a phenomenon that the Holy Spirit is able to do. He is the orchestrator. He is the choreographer. The Holy Spirit choreographs worship on the earth.

A WORSHIP WORKSHOP
WITH ANGELS

By Georgian Banov

I WAS MINISTERING AT the Healing Rooms, a prayer and healing ministry based in Vancouver, British Columbia. The band playing with me was not that good from a technical, musical standpoint, but they were together in the Spirit. Several pastors were there who represented the fivefold ministry, and there was an unusual unity. I was thinking, "Wow, this is great!"

I started leading the worship, and we began with a song I felt particularly strong about. Then I found myself going into another melody, then it shifted again and I felt very strongly to move into a different melody. I was not changing from song to song but from melody to melody. We went on and on—different sounds, different melodies, different rhythms, always changing. It was very free as we went from one to the next, and for about an hour we did one song with all these different variations. It felt really great! The atmosphere was the atmosphere of heaven, and we enjoyed every bit of it.

At the end I sat down, and during the offering a prophetess stood up at the front of the room and said, "Wow, Georgian, I often see angels in this room, but I have never seen Jesus come in. When you started singing, the angels were already here, but then Jesus walked in and He went directly up to you. He was singing melodies in your ear, and you heard it; you picked up on it, and you started singing that melody.

"The angels exclaimed, 'Wow, Lord, how did You do that?' Because they knew you weren't hearing Him with your natural ears. Yet, you changed the melody according to what He would sing to you, over and over again. He would change and sing a new melody, and then you would change and sing the new one. And then He began to tap a different rhythm and you changed to the new rhythm.

"The whole experience was a workshop for the angels to see how the Lord leads you by His Spirit. It's so amazing. We think the angels know it all, but in a sense they are always in amazement of what God does and how He does it. So we just witnessed a workshop for the angels, with God using you, Georgian, as the way of Him showing the angels how He leads by the Spirit."

SINGING WITH ANGELS

By Georgian Banov

ONCE WHEN I was leading worship in England a very unusual thing happened. I was singing and could hear myself in stereo. I was thinking, "Wow, this is like a sound effect." I looked at my stuff, my instruments and audio equipment, but it was all OK; nobody was touching it.

I was singing and singing, and I could hear this stereo effect really strong. I was asking, "Lord, what is this?" I was expecting to hear another voice, a different voice from my own, as if another person was singing with me, but the Lord told me, "I'm singing. I'm singing through you. You're expecting to hear another voice, but this is My voice singing through your voice. I'm singing with you and through you."

I found myself suddenly becoming very self-conscious. I couldn't tell if I was following His vocal lead, or if He was following mine. I couldn't tell who was leading because I could hear the two voices but both were my own voice in stereo. So as I was singing, it was hard to tell which one was me and which one was the Lord singing with and through me. When I started to concentrate on the voices, trying to figure out who was who, I would lose concentration.

Losing concentration during worship actually happens to me often because when I hear the angels singing, I stop thinking about what I'm singing so I can listen to them. This happens almost all the time because I hear the angels all the time.

Those are my precious moments because I can feel people in the audience coming into the heavens, into the atmosphere of the supernatural. When I hear the angels, that's a sure sign to me that I am helping the audience break through into the supernatural, heavenly realm.

FRANKINCENSE, MYRRH, ROSES, AND VANILLA

By Faytene Grasseschi

ALL THE MANIFESTATIONS of the kingdom of heaven—of the supernatural, of the angelic—are mysteries. I just love when they happen, though, because it is so encouraging!

Often I have been in a meeting when everyone experiences the sudden manifestation of angelic winds. I can just be sitting in a chair, and all of a sudden there are gusts of wind, out of nowhere. Or I have been ministering over people, and there comes a supernatural-wind atmosphere, with winds that often are accompanied by a fragrance like frankincense or myrrh. I have smelled the fragrances of roses and vanilla.

I don't know what it is all about, but it does feel nice. And it's not like I'm looking for or seeking after these manifestations. I'm just looking for Jesus. But it is amazing that, when you are in the middle of just walking in the kingdom, the kingdom manifests.

ANGELS RELEASED
WHILE GIVING

By Faytene Grasseschi

O NE OF THE funniest times I have encountered angels was in the form of wind. It was also probably the most intense experience I have had.

It happened when my husband, Robert John, and I were just engaged and decided to tithe together jointly for the first time. Though we were not married, we decided we would make our first tithe, our first gift, together. It happened on a supernormal day. We were at his mom's house, in the basement working at the computer. We decided to give to a ministry online, and it was pretty routine. We went to the ministry's website, clicked "Donate Now," and literally in that very moment it was as if somebody dropped fans into the room. It was as if suddenly all these high-powered fans started blowing.

It was a really intense encounter with the wind of heaven!

These winds were ripping through the room, and instantly we felt filled and refreshed with the Holy Spirit and God's joy. There was an intense sense of God's pleasure with our unity, our unity in giving and our unity in giving to the kingdom. Because God loves it all—He loves our unity, He loves giving, and He definitely loved what the ministry that we gave to was doing. He loved where our first tithe was going.

We were experiencing the joy and pleasure of the Lord. But there was also a sense that something was activated by that act of giving. We know from the Word that angels are dispatched on assignment. God gives angels assignments, and we had a sense that angels were being dispatched in that moment. There was a connection to this action we had just taken as a couple, and now the angels were going to carry out the assignment on our behalf.

And we know from the Bible that there is a principle of sowing and reaping. We weren't sowing just for a reaping, just for a release, we were doing it because we love God and we love to give. But what unfolded in the next couple of weeks was—I want to call it *para-normal* because it was not normal at all.

Shortly after this experience I went to speak at a conference, and it was just nine days before we were to get married. And for Robert John and I, even our wedding was a step of faith. We were going to be newlyweds, and we were paying for the entire wedding ourselves. We were simply trusting God to cover the bills.

So at this conference, completely unprompted, one of the other speakers gets up and announces that I am getting married in nine days. It was just a fun moment. But afterward a couple who had traveled there all the way from Ireland came up to me and said, "Faytene, while that minister was sharing about you getting mar-ried, we really felt like we wanted to sow into the beginning of this new phase in life for you and your husband. If we want to make out a check, where would we make it out, who would we make it out to?"

I was very humbled and had no idea what they were going to do, but I gave them my bank information, and they ended up wiring ten thousand dollars into our new beginning. We were, like, "*Whoa!* This is wild!"

It was the blessing of our Father in heaven who wanted to bless us at the beginning of our new phase.

Looking back, I believe there was something dispatched in the spirit realm through that joint act of giving, that first tithe we made as a couple. For me the manifestation of the wind is a confirmation of that. It was a fruit of the Father's goodness being poured out on us. We were able not only to get married but also to get married with our entire wedding completely paid for.

I believe the angels were involved in administrating that blessing!

ANGELS ARE DRAWN TO WORSHIP

By Melissa Fisher

A NGELS ARE ATTRACTED to a heavenly atmosphere, I believe, because when we go deep into worship or into really high praise, they tend to show up. This makes sense when we think about what praise does. By its very nature praise clears the atmosphere for the presence of heaven to come. When we praise, the atmosphere is cleared for the presence of heaven to fall, and the angels come.

We are called to bring heaven to earth. Jesus taught us this principle in the Lord's Prayer (Matt. 6:9–13). We are supposed to live on earth as they do in heaven.

When we bring heaven to earth, angels are attracted. It feels like home for them. I think it just makes a nice, comfortable place for them to be, and I really believe they like being with us as we are praising.

Angels praise all day long. They love to praise the Lord. When they get around us as we are worshipping God and loving what we do, they are drawn to that and want to come and join in that praise with us.

WE ALL HEARD THE ANGELS SINGING

By Michael Maiden

ONE RECENT, WONDERFUL Sunday morning during worship, we had an angelic visitation at our church. The worship team was leading the congregation, and at a very holy moment all the instruments stopped playing. The congregation was still vocally worshipping the Lord, but all of a sudden the entire worship team fell prostrate. They all lay on their faces.

Seven or eight minutes into this, the congregation was still worshipping. Then all of a sudden there was a glorious high-pitched sound of worship. It was just so extraordinary, beyond human sounding. It was a beautiful angelic sound, and it lasted five or six minutes straight. It was constant. It was a beautiful pitch that mixed in with our worship, just covering it, adding to it.

The next day I had probably two hundred messages from people asking, "Pastor, did you hear the angels at church yesterday?" Yes, I had heard the sound, and I knew it was not human. It truly was an angelic moment.

In fact, a couple thousand people heard it and were really sensitized to what it was, that it was angelic. We had been allowed to hear the angels worshipping with us. There was a ripping of the barrier between the natural and the spirit realms. We had heard them enter our world as we entered theirs. There was a mixture of the two realms in our worship to heaven. It was very, very special.

SEVEN HUNDRED PEOPLE HEARD THE ANGEL

By David Herzog

I HAVE BEEN HAVING angelic experiences since I was a kid. But the one that really marked me was in about 1999 when I was with Ruth Heflin, the Pentecostal evangelist and revivalist, in Ashton, Virginia. I was preaching, and at one point I could discern when angels were there and when they were not. I announced, "There's a huge angel here, and it is coming to help with revival." Revival was already breaking out, and he had come to help.

When I made the announcement no one was at the keyboard or at a microphone leading worship because I was preaching. But all of a sudden I heard a sound, someone singing "*Ooooh.*" It freaked me out! It freaked us all out—everyone there heard it! About seven hundred people were there, at an outdoor amphitheater, and all seven hundred of them heard it.

I stopped preaching and didn't know what to do. I knew I had heard the angel I had just mentioned, the one coming to help with revival, and now he was singing audibly. He wasn't singing just in the spirit realm, though, because it wasn't just me or a few of us who heard him. He was signing audibly, and everyone could hear him.

So I waited until the singing stopped, and then I said the dumbest thing, because I was thinking about what some skeptics might be thinking. After this amazing audible song from the angel, I said, "I don't think that was a train because I don't think there is a train track nearby. I think that was an angel." Such a dumb thing to say after such a major experience.

I looked over at Ruth sitting in the front, but for her the angelic was normal. She lived in that realm, so she was nonchalant about it. But for me at the time, it was not normal. It really marked me.

194

THE ANGELS SANG WITH US

By Stephanie Herzog

WE WERE DOING a series of meetings with pastor and church planter Randy DeMain, and we hit this level in worship, this realm, where the angels wanted to join in! It was so amazing—all the instruments had stopped playing, but you could hear this sound, a really high-pitched sound. It's hard to explain, but it was as if you could hear singing. We were hearing the angels worshipping God, and it changed the whole atmosphere of the room.

For me it really was like I had died and gone to heaven. I didn't want to move. I was just listening to the singing. Then something else came into the room—it was an awe of God. When the awe of God comes and you can hear the angels singing, it takes worship to an entirely new level. It becomes more like spirit-to-spirit worship. It takes you to another place.

At one point the angels also released heavenly fragrances. I was preaching at this point and speaking on how God likes it when we die to our flesh, that He loves the smell of marinated, barbecued flesh. And that's when we all smelled it!

A sudden smell of garlic filled the room. Of course, we all were thinking that someone there had garlic bread or Italian food in their bag because it was a really strong smell. So we asked, but nobody did. We even checked with the hotel's kitchen to see if they were cooking anything, but no. Yet there was a strong smell of garlic filling the room.

I believe the angels brought it and released it. It was God confirming the message about His liking the smell of barbecued flesh! That might sound weird, but we cannot put in a box what God, the Holy Spirit, and the angels do.

MESSENGERS OF FIRE

By Steve Swanson

I AM A WORSHIP leader, and occasionally during worship I see things in the spirit realm. It doesn't happen very often, but I remember one time in particular. We were recording the live CD *Messengers of Fire*, which ironically is about angels.

I was on stage at my keyboards, singing and leading the people in worship. During that session I kept seeing orange and yellow lights. We were recording the CD live at this event, and I was wondering if somehow those lights were going to ruin the recording. But we kept singing while the lights kept going, and I could hear people going, "*Aahh!*"

While I watched these lights, I saw them going into people. They would circle around the sanctuary then go into people. Then, as the lights would go into people, they would go, "*Aahh!*"

I spontaneously started to sing about it. I sang: "Ribbons of light, ribbons of light! Going in and going in, ascending and descending." The music was simply reflecting the movement of the lights, but then it was as if the lights responded and joined in the worship.

I believe the angels do worship with us. They are our fellow servants of God. We both worship Him together. In fact, I have noticed that when the angels are present and they worship with us, there is an extra *umph*, an extra anointing in the room. This was one of those times!

Later, after the recording session, one of the other worship leaders told me she also saw angels enter the room. She was on the other side of the platform and did not know what I had seen. She said the angels had gifts and were putting the gifts into people, and as they entered people, the gifts became unwrapped.

So what I saw as ribbons of light she saw as gifts going into people and being unwrapped. The fact that we both sensed the presence of the angels in that worship session, and that we both saw something going into people and blessing them, was a confirmation to me that what I had seen was real.

I have experienced angels joining us in worship a lot. I have noticed that they seem to like warfare worship. They also seem to respond to certain sounds that I play on my keyboard, particularly angelic sounds. I like to incorporate synthesizer sounds in worship, specifically angelic, heavenly sounds, because angels seem to inhabit those sounds at times.

I really like to create that kind of atmosphere in worship because when the angels come, they bring healing, deliverance, and salvation. The angels are sent to minister to the heirs of salvation (Heb. 1:14), and as we all gather in worship of the Most High and there is an angelic presence in the room, people get healed, delivered, and set free.

Now that's my kind of worship!

I SCREAMED LIKE A LITTLE GIRL!

By Steven Springer

I HAVE HAD SEVERAL experiences in which I am lying in bed, praying in the Spirit, and all of a sudden I am pulled up, out of my body, into the spiritual realm. One night when that happened, I was suddenly pulled up into a room. It was all white. Suddenly, massive doors, twenty feet high, opened in front of me, and I was invited to go into a room that was full of angels.

As I went in, the angels suddenly began coming up into my face to look at me, as if to say, "Who is this guy?" One by one they would look at me, then *whoosh*, take off. The next one would come up to me, then *whoosh*; then the next one, *whoosh*; and then the next one. Each would examine me, and then *whoosh*, he would take off—one after another after another.

Then two came into my face, and they smiled, then suddenly stepped back and bowed down. They were not bowing to me; they were bowing before an intense light and warmth and a presence. I began to feel it coming toward me. I could feel the presence coming toward me. I realized it was Jesus, and His arms were opened up for me.

There was a radiating light coming out of Him, and His robe and garments looked alive as He got closer. His robes were simultaneously white and multicolored. They had the appearance of clothing but also, at the same time, looked much more like a living organism. And the closer He got to me, the more it felt like the pressing of His presence was too much. I began to scream. In fact, I screamed like a little girl, "*Arh!*"

I really thought I was going to die. I remember just screaming out and screaming out and screaming out. I felt as if I was going to be crushed by His presence. It was a fear of the Lord that overcame me.

The next thing I knew, I was back in my room. My first thought was, "No! That was Jesus. I want to go back!"

I understand now what the apostle John was talking about in Revelation 1:17: "When I saw Him, I fell at His feet as dead." When you are in the presence of Jesus, even in the presence of His angels, you can feel this "I'm going to die" sense because He is so overwhelming. It was His love; I was so overwhelmed by His love that I could not contain it. It is amazing!

The crazy thing is that when I was first saved, I thought everyone had these kinds of experiences. So I would share them as if they were normal, and people would look at me and ask, "Are you on drugs?" I was insistent: "No, I haven't done drugs in, like, five months!" I was not on some drug-induced trip. I was literally seeing these things with my physical eyes. The unseen realm was opened up to me.

It was a gift to me, and it is part of the gift of discernment—to be able to know and to discern. But my experiences in the gift went beyond just a simple feeling to the point that I knew in my gut. For me a veil was pulled back, and I was allowed to see into the spirit realm. I was able to see both the warring of dark spirits and the spirits of light. I could see the converging, colliding war.

MY FAVORITE ANGEL STORY

By James Goll

I HAVE A FAVORITE angelic story from the Bible. Put all the angel stories together, and this one outweighs them all! It goes something like this:

> There was a man named Jesus. He told His disciples that He was going to be crucified, that He would die and be buried, but on the third day He would rise from the dead. Well, He was in fact crucified; He died and was buried. On the morning of the third day two women went out to His tomb. There they were met by an angel, who spoke this to them: "The man you are seeking is not here. He has risen."
>
> —MARK 16, AUTHOR'S PARAPHRASE

These two women ran and told the disciples of Jesus what they had encountered and what the angel said. The angel proclaiming the resurrection of the Messiah—now that's an angelic encounter!

James W. Goll (www.JamesGoll.com) is the president of Encounters Network, the director of Prayer Storm, and the director of God Encounters Training—an eSchool of the Heart. He is also a member of the Harvest International Ministries apostolic team and an instructor in the Wagner Leadership Institute. With great joy James has shared Jesus in more than fifty nations teaching and imparting the power of intercession, prophetic ministry, and life in the Spirit. He is the author of numerous books, including The Seer, The Lost Art of Intercession, *and* Angelic Encounters: Engaging Help From Heaven. *James was married for thirty-two years before his wife and ministry partner, Michal Ann, graduated to heaven in the fall of 2008. He lives in Franklin, Tennessee, and has four adult children who all love Jesus.*

Conclusion

WHAT NOW?

By Jonathan Nixon

IN THE PRECEDING pages you read stories about messenger angels, guardian and protecting angels, military angels, singing angels, warring angels, rescue angels, and angels releasing fire, healing, and deliverance. These angelic messengers are partnering with God to accomplish His will in the earth and in our lives. But as my friend James Goll wrote, there is one angel story that tops them all. It is the story of the angels announcing the coming of the promised Messiah.

> It is through Jesus, not angels, that we are saved from sin and reconciled with the Father. It is through Him that our lives are made new. We may marvel at the things angels know, the places they can be, the feats they can accomplish that are beyond our limited human ability. But what excites angels? Luke 15:10 says "there is joy in the presence of the angels of God over one sinner who repents."

The angels want you to turn toward heaven. They want you to accept Jesus as your Lord, because when you do, God activates them to do their job. When you become an heir of salvation, the angels of heaven are commissioned by God Himself to guard, protect, assist, and bless you with all that heaven has planned for you.

There is a war raging between heaven and earth, and sometimes it seems as if the devil controls the system and has all the power and advantage. The Bible says he controls principalities, powers, and dominions. But we must not become so busy with counting demons that we forget the angels.

The Bible teaches that God will use His mighty angels to execute judgment and totally eliminate Satan from the universe. Revelation 20:1–3 says: "Then I saw an angel coming down from heaven, having the key to the bottomless pit and a great chain in his hand. He laid hold of the dragon, that serpent of old, who is the Devil and Satan, and bound him for a thousand years; and he cast him into the bottomless pit, and shut him up, and set a seal on him, so that he should deceive the nations no more."

Think about it. Right now we are encompassed by a heavenly host so powerful that we need not fear the spiritual war raging around us. We can boldly face Satan and his legions with all the confidence of the grizzled, old Army captain who, when told that he and his men were surrounded by the enemy, shouted, "Good, don't let any of the enemy escape!" Lift up your eyes and see, as Elisha's servant did, that the angels of God are ready to go to battle on your behalf. (See 2 Kings 6:16–17.)

All we need do is press in and get into alignment with the plans and strategy of heaven. How do we do this? I press into the presence of God. I seek after Him, not angels. When I sense the presence of angels or, perhaps, when I actually see them, I ask God, "Why are these angels here, Lord? Are they bringing me a message? Are they here to protect me in a battle? Are they bringing me something that I need to achieve a kingdom assignment?" Then I listen for an answer and obey.

God sends His angels to us because He loves us. He built the natural and the supernatural world around us and for us. Remember, He created us. He made us in His image. We are His best work, His masterpiece. Genesis 1:31 says, "Then God saw everything that He had made, and indeed it was very good."

God wants a relationship with us. He wants to provide for us. He wants to bless us. And He sends His angels to do just that—to bless us!

We have a supernatural God who wants to be our closest friend. He sends His supernatural angels to bring us messages; to guard us, protect us, sing to us, and do battle for us; to bring us holiness and fire; and to heal us, deliver us, rescue us, and minister to us. All we have to say is, "Yes, God!"—and hang on for the ride of our lives.

From Jonathan Nixon, author of *Angel Stories*:

The life of Jesus Christ was a mystical adventure.
He turned water into wine, He walked on water, He appeared and disappeared,
He walked through walls, He rose from the dead.

The life of a Jesus follower can also be this same kind of mystical adventure.
John 14:12 reads, "I tell you the truth, anyone who believes in me
will do the same works I have done, and even greater works" (NLT).

This is not merely a suggestion, it is a challenge and a direction to those who
believe in God to do not only the same things that Jesus did, but also to do
even greater!

I created Tentmaker Film Company with a mission to explore these
spiritual and supernatural truths to learn how we all can live our everyday in this
kind of mystical life. Through both documentary films and books, I want to
explore the supernatural phenomenon that Jesus, the Old Testament prophets,
and New Testament disciples walked in as a regular part of their life.
Upcoming Tentmaker Film Company projects include:
- *Understanding Dreams and Visions;*
- *Modern Day Prophets;*
- *Portals to Heaven*, and more.

Find these and more at www.TentmakerFilmCompany.com.

Jonathan is married to Elizabeth A. Nixon, Esq., author of
Inspired by the Psalms: Decrees That Renew Your Heart and Mind.
They have been married for 28 years and have a 5-year-old son, Joshua.
Together they all enjoy sailing catamarans and off-road Jeep adventures.

EMPOWERED
TO RADICALLY CHANGE
YOUR WORLD

Charisma House brings you books, e-books, and other media from dynamic Spirit-filled Christians who are passionate about God.

Check out all of our releases from best-selling authors like **Jentezen Franklin**, **Perry Stone**, and **Kimberly Daniels** and experience God's supernatural power at work.

CHARISMA
HOUSE

www.charismahouse.com
twitter.com/charismahouse • facebook.com/charismahouse